The Reminiscences

of

Mr. George C. Cooper

Member of the Golden Thirteen

Copyright © 1989
U.S. Naval Institute
Annapolis, Maryland

Preface

In 1986, at the suggestion of Lieutenant Mark Crayton, USN, of the naval recruiting command at Great Lakes, Illinois, the Naval Institute began a project to record the memories of the eight surviving members of the Golden Thirteen. The initial round of interviews with the Navy's first black officers was conducted between October 1986 and January 1987. Excerpts were published in the May 1987 Naval Review issue of the Proceedings. Mr. Cooper then suggested the advisability of doing a second round of interviews after the men of the Golden Thirteen had a chance to read each other's transcripts and give further thought to the subject. Mr. Cooper's was the first interview in the second round, and his is the first transcript to be completed and made public.

During his professional career, George Cooper has waged a personal campaign on behalf of racial enlightenment and cooperation. In the memoir that follows he cites examples of the ways in which he fostered understanding, both through deliberate attempts to relate to other people and unconsciously through the manner in which he has lived his life. The qualities he has demonstrated throughout his lifetime were passed on by his parents when he was growing up in the small town of Washington, North Carolina, in the 1920s and 1930s. From his father he learned the importance of education and the need to produce something that people are willing to pay for in the marketplace. From his mother he learned humanity and the quality of caring for people in all walks of life.

Following his education at Hampton Institute in Virginia, Mr. Cooper was in business for himself briefly, then worked for the National Youth Administration and as a civilian instructor at the naval training station at Hampton during World War II. In 1943 he enlisted in the Navy with an appointment as chief petty officer, and in early 1944 he was one of 16 black enlisted men chosen to undergo officer candidate training at Great Lakes, Illinois. In this memoir he describes the practices by which the white instructors often worked at cross purposes from the Navy's institutional goal of commissioning black men. He describes the pressure under which the 16 men worked, for they were representing not just themselves but the more than 100,000 black personnel in the Navy of that time. After he became an officer, Mr. Cooper returned to Hampton and worked under the enlightened leadership of Commander Edwin H. Downes.

In the years since World War II, Mr. Cooper has had a distinguished career in the civilian world. He served on the faculty at Hampton Institute; developed a home-cleaning service in Ohio; worked in the city government of Dayton, Ohio, as a housing inspector, city planner, and division director; and headed Antioch College's international work-study program. In the years since retirement, Mr. Cooper has been active in a job training program to foster economic opportunities for black workers in Dayton, and he has served as president of the Dayton chapter of the Navy League. Throughout all these activities, he has demonstrated a talent for working with people and moving them toward common goals.

The interviews in this oral history were transcribed by Ms. Deborah Reid, formerly of the Naval Institute. Mr. Cooper has done some minor editing of the transcript in the interests of clarity and smoothness.

                                          Paul Stillwell
                                          Director of Oral History
                                          U. S. Naval Institute
                                          January 1989

George Clinton Cooper was born in Washington, North Carolina on 7 September 1916, the son of Edward L. and Laura J. Cooper. He attended public schools in Washington, and graduated from Hampton [Virginia] Institute in 1939 with a bachelor of science degree in trade education. In 1948 he received his master's degree in personnel administration from Columbia University in New York.

After graduation from Hampton Institute, Mr. Cooper first worked in his father's sheet-metal shop in Washington. After six months, he opened his own shop in Wilson, North Carolina, where he served as production foreman from September 1939 to January 1941.

In 1941 he became a sheet-metal instructor for the War Manpower Commission at Wilberforce [Ohio] University. He reamined there until June 1942, when he accepted a similar position at the naval training station at Hampton Institute. He enlisted in the Navy in June 1943 with a direct appointment as a chief petty officer, and remained as an instructor at Hampton until February 1944.

In January 1944 he was among 16 men chosen to comprise the Navy's first officer training class for blacks. In March, 12 of this group were commissioned as ensigns, and one as a warrant officer.

Ensign Cooper reported back to the naval training station at Hampton Institute in March 1944, and served as personnel officer and training supervisor there until September

1945 when he resigned his commission for health reasons. He remained at Hampton as a civilian in the position of chairman of the trades training department until February 1952.

For the next three years, Mr. Cooper worked as vice president in charge of personnel and sales for Finer Services, Inc., a comprehensive interior decorating and cleaning firm.

From February 1955 until July 1964, Cooper worked for the City of Dayton, Ohio, as a housing inspector (1955 to 1957), an associate planner (1957 to 1962), and a housing expeditor (1962 to 1964).

In July 1964, Mr. Cooper accepted a position as the associate director of the extramural department at Antioch College in Yellow Springs, Ohio, where he was in charge of the student work-study program. From 1966 to 1970 he was the director of the international work-study program at Antioch.

From September 1970 until his retirement in July 1981, he returned to the city government of Dayton, where he served as director of the Department of Human Resources.

A long-time proponent of racial cooperation and economic opportunities for the poor, Mr. Cooper has remained active in community affairs. He has served as president of both the Dayton chapter of the Navy League and the Supporting Council on Preventive Effort (CAP), and as chairman of the Housing Task Force of the City of Dayton. He was vice president of the Dayton Council on Alcoholism and Drug Abuse and a member of Housing Now, Inc. He was a member of the board of directors of the Dayton Council on World Affairs and on the board of trustees of the University of Dayton and the Dayton Art Institute. He was secretary-treasurer of the Supervisory Council on Crime and Juvenile Delinquency and on the executive committee of the Dayton Area Council on Alcoholism and Drug Abuse.

Mr. Cooper is currently the president of both the Dayton Fund for Home Rehabilitation and the Wegerzyn Horticulture Center; chairman of both the Institutional Racism Project (Episcopal Diocese of Southern Ohio) and the Dayton/Monrovia Sister City Committee; a member of the board of directors of the Human Services Levy Council; a member of the Community Affairs Committee; and honorary chair of the Dayton Black Cultural Festival.

Authorization

The U. S. Naval Institute is hereby authorized to make available to individuals, libraries, and other repositories of its choosing the transcripts of two oral history interviews concerning the life and career of the undersigned. The interviews were recorded on 15 October 1986 and 18 July 1988 in collaboration with Paul Stillwell for the U. S. Naval Institute.

The undersigned does hereby release and assign to the U. S. Naval Institute all right, title, restrictions, and interest in the interviews. The copyright in both the oral and transcribed versions shall be the sole property of the U. S. Naval Institute. The tape recordings of the interviews are and will remain the property of the U. S. Naval Institute.

Signed and sealed this ___18th___ day of ___January___ 1989.

_____
Mr. George C. Cooper

Interview Number 1 with Mr. George C. Cooper

Place: Mr. Cooper's home in Dayton, Ohio
Date: Wednesday, 15 October 1986
Interviewer: Paul Stillwell

Q: To begin at the beginning, Mr. Cooper, could you tell me something about when and where you were born and what you remember about your parents and your brothers and sisters?

Mr. Cooper: I was born in a little town, Washington, North Carolina, on the seventh of September in 1916.* I was one of a family of 11 children, one of whom died shortly after birth, so we came up in a family of ten kids. My father was a sheet-metal worker by trade, and in the early part of my life, worked for a white shop in this little town.** As I understand it, he went in one day and said to his boss that he had this big family, he had to make more money, and he'd like a raise. The man told him he could not afford to give him a raise, so my father said, "Well, in that case, I've enjoyed working here. Thank you for the opportunity you have given me, but I think I'll start my own shop."

According to the story, the man said to him, "There's

---
*Census figures for Washington, North Carolina, were as follows: 1910: 6,211; 1920: 6,314; 1930: 7,035; 1940: 8,569.
**Edward L. Cooper was George Cooper's father.

if you think you can do it, I will even help you. Go back in the shop, and if you find some pieces that in your judgment are obsolete or stuff that we no longer use, if you think that you can use it, you can have it." It was this kind of a relationship between employer and employee. He did, in fact, start his own business.

Q: Where did you fit in the sequence of children?

Mr. Cooper: Number eight out of 11, one having died. Out of that shop my father saw each of the ten of us at least through college.

Q: It sounds as if he did very well.

Mr. Cooper: In terms of formal education, he stopped school in the third grade. My mother stopped school in the fourth grade.* If I've ever seen a self-educated man, I think my dad was one of them. Very independent, always stressed to each of us, his children, that he felt that the only thing that anybody would pay for in this world was production. If you were not in a position to produce, don't expect too much in return.

He was hell-bent on education, saying, "You've got to have an education, because without it you're simply not

---
*Laura J. Cooper was George Cooper's mother.

going to make it." There was never any question in any of our minds that we were not going to finish high school and go to college. This was just a foregone conclusion. This was a part of coming up in that household. The old homestead is still there. I'm going back next week to touch base with my two oldest sisters, neither of whom ever got married; the rest of us did. They've maintained the homestead and still live there; they're both in their 80s.

I graduated from high school there in little Washington, obviously a segregated high school.

Q: How good an education, would you say in retrospect, that you got there?

Mr. Cooper: Very mediocre. I remember three teachers from primary grade through high school who, in my judgment, were exceptional people, two ladies and a gentleman, who, I think, were largely responsible for influencing much of my educational pursuits and thoughts and that kind of thing.*

Q: Did they have the capacity to inspire as well as educate?

Mr. Cooper: Yes, these three people particularly. I'll
_____
*These three teachers were Miss Rebecca Harvey, Miss Evelyn Evans, and Mr. Cox.

never forget any of the three of them.

Having graduated from high school, I then went to Hampton Institute in Tidewater, Virginia. I went as a work year student. Hampton had a program where you would come in and during the first year take a very light load, maybe six semester hours a semester, because you worked full-time, in an effort to pay your way that year and hopefully have some money to start the following year.

Q: This is the one that Armstrong was connected to.

Mr. Cooper: Yes. General Armstrong had founded the institution.* There's a story about that, too, later on.**

So I went to Hampton. Some of my brothers and sisters were already out of college, and they helped to the extent that they could. My dad helped to the extent that he could.

Q: What was the sort of work you were doing to lay some

---

*Brigadier General Samuel Chapman Armstrong (1839-1893) was colonel of a black regiment in the Civil War, and that led to his interest in vocational education for black students. In 1868 he founded the Hampton Normal and Agricultural Institute. For a book on his life, see Edith Armstrong Talbot, <u>Samuel Chapman Armstrong: A Biographical Study</u> (New York: Doubleday, Page & Company, 1904).
**General Armstrong's son Daniel was involved in training Mr. Cooper and other members of the Golden Thirteen during World War II.

Cooper #1 - 5

money aside?

Mr. Cooper: I worked in a place called Holly Tree Inn, which was the guest facility for the campus, and about half of it was occupied by faculty. I was basically a combination bellman and maid, cleaning up and working in the dining room as a waiter. Subsequently I worked in the student dining room as a waiter to make some money for the rest of my tenure at Hampton. Fortunately, I had a fairly decent singing voice and got to be a member of the Hampton Choir, the Trade School Singers, and the Hampton Student Quartet. This gave me an opportunity to make some money and do a fair amount of travel, because the quartet traveled rather extensively. I was fortunate. I not only got paid for singing in the quartet, but I got paid for driving, because I managed to get the job as chauffeur for the quartet. So I got double pay whenever we were on a trip. Actually, when I left Hampton, I had some money left over.

Q: Were you preparing for a specific career at that point?

Mr. Cooper: Yes. My father, I've indicated, was a sheet-metal worker, and I thought that was what I wanted to do. Hampton, of course, was noted for its trade school. So I went in and took the trade, and then I went on and got a

Cooper #1 - 6

degree in what at that point was called vocational education, because I didn't know whether I'd want to teach it or work at it or what. After I got my degree, I went back to North Carolina to go in business with my dad.

Q: Did you have a fair amount of manual dexterity as well?

Mr. Cooper: There were six boys in the family, and I was the only one who would even know a hammer from a saw. I spent a fair amount of time in the shop with my dad, growing up, so that I can use my hands reasonably well.

Q: Were you in sports in North Carolina and Hampton?

Mr. Cooper: No, no. No sports ever. The nearest I got to sports was being a cheerleader.

Q: What sorts of Jim Crow situations did you encounter in both places?*

Mr. Cooper: Well, of course, in little Washington, we're going back now 60-plus years. Jim Crow was the name of the game. Everything was separate; nothing was equal. I

---

*Thomas D. Rice, a black minstrel singer, wrote a song and dance titled "Jim Crow" in 1832. Later in the century, the term took on the meaning of segregation of the races, as in "Jim Crow laws."

recall sitting up in the balcony at a theater in little Washington, initially doing the same thing at Hampton, in Virginia, in the early stages of my college career.

I got in trouble in little Washington. This connects with the Navy experience. When I was very young, probably eight or nine, I was going downtown. My dad, in addition to having his trade and running the shop, cultivated every vacant lot in a five-block radius of our house. We had a cow. I had to milk the cow twice a day. I had to deliver this milk in the morning, and in season I had to deliver the excess produce from our various gardens to sell to downtown merchants.

On one of these trips taking some stuff downtown, I had a conflict with a little white boy on Market Street. It was the wrong day for him to call me a "nigger," and we had it out. Fortunately, I won the fight, or came out better, obviously, than he did. Nothing resulted from it then. Nobody even saw us. I went on and finished the chore. I subsequently heard from it tangentially, after the kid went back home. His father got in touch with my dad, but nothing really ever came of it--just a fight among kids. It's interesting, though. I don't know how many years later that was thrown back at me at Great Lakes.*

---

*The sequel to this incident is discussed on page 27 of this transcript.

Cooper #1 - 8

Q: I've heard from the others in the group that were at Great Lakes that there were thorough investigations by the FBI.* The knowledge of your fight must have come out of that.

Mr. Cooper: Yes, this documents it.

But back to your question. Segregation was in full swing. There were white and black drinking fountains, white and black sections in the railroad station, the bus station, everything.

Q: And there was no choice but to accept it.

Mr. Cooper: No, you had no choice. You had no choice. The "choice" that you had was to try to make the best of it or get in trouble. And making the best of it did not necessarily mean being subservient, with your hat in your hand, but taking an unfortunate situation and trying to make something creative and constructive out of it. We'll talk more about that in terms of the Navy experience.

Q: Were there other situations in which you walked away from a fight rather than getting involved?

Mr. Cooper: Right. You do this all your life. Yes, you

---
*FBI--Federal Bureau of Investigation.

do this all your life. I had a couple of those experiences in the Navy, one in particular.

Q: Hampton is right near the large naval complex at Norfolk. Did you have any interest or awareness of the Navy at that time?

Mr. Cooper: Yes, tangentially. I've always loved to fish. Even as a student, I would go fishing. We would go out in Hampton Roads. Here's the naval base over here. You could see it from the fishing grounds. So that I was aware of the existence of the Navy but never really considered the Navy as a career. I never even considered going into the Navy.

Q: The range of options was so limited.

Mr. Cooper: Yes, yes.

Q: How was the Navy perceived in the black community in the mid-1930s?

Mr. Cooper: Well, the only thing that a black man could do in the Navy was serve as a steward's mate, and that was the perception. If you wanted to be a steward's mate, the Navy was a good deal for you. But beyond that, there was no chance of anything. The opportunity simply was not there. Hair is much more familiar with it than I am.* He can talk with much more authority about how we understand the Navy decided, finally, to really do something about this business of black officers.

Q: I'm interested in your recollection of that as well-- your interpretation.

Mr. Cooper: The reason I say Hair can do it is that he was a part of it. Hair went to school under Mary McLeod Bethune at Bethune-Cookman College.** Of course, Mrs. Bethune and Mrs. Roosevelt were very close friends.*** Mrs. Bethune, according to information we have, had a great deal of influence in the determination that was made by the Navy, at the insistence of the President, that something be done about this situation. But, again, Hair knows the details of it. He recollects them, because his mind clicks like a clock.

---

*James E. Hair is a member of the Golden Thirteen. During the period when the group of officer candidates was undergoing training in 1944, he spelled his name "Hare" for reasons he explains in his own oral history.
**Mary McLeod Bethune (1875-1955) was a black educator who in 1904 opened at Daytona Beach, Florida, a small school called Daytona Normal and Industrial Institute. It merged in 1923 with Cookman Institute to form Bethune-Cookman College, with Mrs. Bethune as president.
***Eleanor Roosevelt (1884-1962) was the socially conscious wife of President Franklin D. Roosevelt.

Q: I look forward to talking to him.

Did you actually get into the business back in Washington?

Mr. Cooper: Yes, I went back and went into the business with my father. One of the things that we made in the shop were tobacco flues.

Q: What were they?

Mr. Cooper: Down South, you raise tobacco and you cure it in a barn under fire. That fire was made in a little homemade furnace. Off from that furnace, running around the perimeter of the barn on the inside, were sheet metal pipes maybe 15 to 16 inches in diameter, which provided the heat to cure this tobacco that was stacked up maybe a story and a half or two stories. Of course, having taken sheet metal work in the trade school at Hampton, I took drafting and was able to draft whatever I needed. Dad, on the other hand, had a pattern for everything that he made. If he needed to make an elbow and he didn't have a pattern, he'd just take an old elbow and tear it apart and make a pattern from that, and then go ahead and do it. Because I wanted to draft everything and lay it out my way, and he wanted to do it his way, there was something of a conflict. We stayed together for about six months.

Q: What year was that?

Mr. Cooper: 1939-40. At this time, I knew about a black insurance company, North Carolina Mutual Life Insurance Company. They had an appreciable amount of property in Wilson, North Carolina, a little town which was about 50 miles from my home town in Washington, and they needed somebody to come in and do some sheet-metal work for them.* I borrowed my dad's car and went up and checked it out. I discovered that they did, in fact, have a fair amount of property and a fair amount of sheet-metal work that needed to be done. I reasoned that if I could get that contract, that would be a beginning for me to start my own business.

So I went back and talked it over with my dad, and he said, "Go for it. If there's anything in my shop . . ." He told me again the story about how his shop started, and I took a lot of stuff out of his shop and started this little business.

What I wanted to do ultimately was to start manufacturing sheet-metal caskets. At that point in my life, it was impossible for me to get the kind of financing I needed for the kind of equipment that I needed to do this. I was, however, able to get enough work to keep the

---
*The census of 1940 reported a population of 19,234 for Wilson, North Carolina.

shop open.

Q: What sorts of things would an insurance company need in the way of sheet-metal?

Mr. Cooper: They use an awful lot of metal roofs in eastern North Carolina, and that was primarily what I was doing for them--roofing and gutters. They must have had 75 or 80 pieces of property there. Something was continuously going wrong with them. So with that as a base, I was able to start a business in that little community. There had been no black sheet-metal worker there.

That same year, 1939, I married Margarett Gillespie of Hamilton, Ohio. My wife got a job as librarian in the high school in Wilson, and there are a lot of interesting tales related to that, related to discrimination and that kind of thing. One of the stories that she remembers is that when she went there, the principal of the high school said, "I'm going to bring the superintendent in to meet you tomorrow, and don't be surprised when he calls you Margarett."

She said, "Well, when he calls me Margarett, he's going to be horribly surprised because I'm going to ask him his first name and tell him if he can call me Margarett, I'm going to call him by his first name."

Mr. Edward Barnes, the principal, said, "Oh, my God,

you can't do that. We just don't operate like that." He said, "You northerners are going to come down here and just ruin things for us."

She said, "Well, Mr. Barnes, if you think that he's going to call me 'Margarett' and it's going to create a problem, don't bring him in tomorrow."

He did, in fact, bring the man in, and for some unknown reason he called her "Mrs. Cooper." He addressed her as "Mrs. Cooper" the whole time she was there, and, to her knowledge, called everybody else by their first names. What happened, I don't know.

Q: If you demand respect, you get it.

Mr. Cooper: But she never told the superintendent that.

Q: The word got back to him.

Mr. Cooper: I don't know how the word got back to him, but that's an interesting little sidelight.

As I say, I really wanted to go into the manufacturing of caskets, but I couldn't swing it. We were making enough to live on, between her job and mine, but by this time, it was beginning to get hard to get metal to do the kind of work I was doing. You could get metal if you were doing defense work, but for maintenance and upkeep of houses, I found it difficult to get the materials that I needed to work with. At this time, NYA was coming into focus. Do you know what NYA is?

Q: No.

Mr. Cooper: National Youth Administration, a federal program for training young people, ostensibly for defense work. Somewhere I saw an ad in the paper that they needed a sheet-metal instructor at an NYA facility that had opened up at Wilberforce University in Ohio.* My wife had gone to college there. So I said, "Well, let's check this out." I wrote and got some information and applications, sent the application in, and was invited out for an interview to teach aircraft sheet-metal work.

So I walked into the man's office, and he said, "Mr. Cooper, somebody made a mistake."

I said, "What do you mean, somebody made a mistake?"

He said, "We thought you were white. I'm going to be perfectly honest with you."

I said, "I thought you were looking for a sheet-metal instructor."

He said, "We are. I'm going to be honest with you again. I've never seen a black sheet-metal worker. I just don't believe you can do the job."

───────────
*Wilberforce University, Wilberforce, Ohio, about a dozen miles east of Dayton.

I said, "Well, you have my credentials in front of you. Obviously I didn't fabricate these things. I at least know how to spell sheet metal. And I've come a long way." Because from Wilson, North Carolina, to Dayton, Ohio, at that point in time was a pretty good little trip.

Q: At your expense.

Mr. Cooper: At my expense.

So he said, "You have, in fact, come a long way. I'll tell you what I'll do. I don't really believe you can do this job, but we have a fully equipped shop here. I will give you a set of blueprints for a simple thing like a metal locker, and if you can make one in a week, I'll give you the job."

I said, "That's a good deal." I said, "I don't really think it's fair, but if that's what it takes to get this job, to find out whether or not I'm qualified for it, I'll go for it."

Two days later, I called him and asked him to come look at this locker. Interestingly enough, the basic piece of equipment that I needed for the manufacture of caskets was the basic piece of equipment that you needed to make metal lockers, and he had this piece of equipment in the shop. I had never had one in my hand before, but we made that locker in two days working with three students who had been there with the prior instructor. I called the gentleman from Columbus and told him he could come and look at the locker. He said, "I thought you were going to take a week to do it."

I said, "No, that was your suggestion. I didn't say how long it was going to take me to do it."

So he came and looked at it. And to make a long story short, I got the job.

Then World War II started breathing down our necks, and I got an opportunity to apply for a job at a naval training station at Hampton Institute in Tidewater, Virginia, to teach metalsmiths in a Class A training school. So I said to Peg, "This is an opportunity to get back to Hampton [where I'd done my undergraduate work], and it might keep me out of the service for two or three years."

Q: By then the people at Wilberforce were probably sorry to see you go.

Mr. Cooper: Yes. We decided we would go for it. I applied for the job and went down for an interview. The skipper at the naval training school was a Commander

Cooper #1 - 18

Downes.* He was gruff; that was the initial impression I had of him. Very matter of fact, strictly business.

Q: Was this around 1941-42?

Mr. Cooper: Yes, in the fall of '42. Commander Downes said, "Mr. Cooper, we would like to have you take this job, because we need you, and there aren't many of you around, white or colored. And if you take the job, I'll see what I can do to keep you from being drafted. I can't promise you anything obviously, but I do know we need you here. And what you can do here may have a little bit more weight than what you're doing at Wilberforce in terms of keeping you in your civilian capacity."

I said, "Fine. Let's go for it." So I went there and started training metalsmiths for the Navy in this Class A training school which had been set up; it was an all-black school. At that point in time, ship's company was 80% to 85% white. Very few blacks. And about half the civilian instructors were black, the other half white. So we went to work there.

---
*Edwin Hall Downes (1897-1976) was graduated from the Naval Academy in the class of 1920. He resigned as an ensign in 1922 and earned a master's degree in education from Columbia University. In 1941 he was recalled to active duty as a Naval Reserve lieutenant, promoted to lieutenant commander in 1942, and commander in 1943. After his period of duty at the naval training station at Hampton, Virginia, he was assigned to the U. S. Naval Mission Peru, where he was dean of the faculty at the Peruvian Naval Academy.

One day Commander Downes came in, and he said, "I want you to go to Great Lakes. I can't keep you out any longer." He said, "But if you will sign up for the Navy, I don't think you'll be sorry. You've got to go somewhere pretty soon. I've checked it out thoroughly. You've either got to go in the Army, the Air Force, or the Navy. You've got to go somewhere. I can't hold onto you any longer. But if you'll agree to go into the Navy, I think I can guarantee you chief petty officer right off the bat. And I think I can bring you back here to do the same job you're doing now."

I said, "Well, that's a winner. Let's go." And that's how I got into the Navy on 22 June 1943.

Q: Frank Sublett mentioned Commander Downes also.*

Mr. Cooper: Yes. He was quite a guy. I'll tell you more about him later on in this story. Commander Downes could walk through at inspection--and I forget how many people we had in training at Hampton, 300 or 400, probably--and he'd call 60% of them by their name. You'd have a new company coming in, say, on a weekend, and he would inspect them that weekend. He'd call a third of them by their last names the next time he inspected them. Fantastic memory.

---

*Frank E. Sublett, Jr., is a member of the Golden Thirteen. His recollections of Downes are contained in his own oral history.

This makes an impression on anybody. You just meet me today and then you see me a week later and say, "Hi, George." I mean, it impresses the hell out of me or you or anybody else. Well, this guy had a way with him, and he just knew how to win friends and influence people, despite the fact that he was all strictly business. No monkey business at all, in any shape, form, or fashion.

We helped train some metalsmiths for the Navy. I went into the service and got the chief petty officer rating and came back to the same job and actually did the same thing until I went to Great Lakes.

Q: How long were you at Great Lakes? Was that the boot camp period?

Mr. Cooper: I didn't go to boot camp. I just signed some papers, and I was a chief petty officer. No boot camp, no anything. I went right back to work at Hampton the next day in the same job. So then we got to go to Great Lakes in early 1944, and I knew the day that I left Hampton that I was going to Great Lakes to go to officer candidate school, or at least to be interviewed for officer candidate school, because I didn't know then that the selection had been made. It was very hush-hush.

So I went up to Great Lakes and ran into the rest of

these men who were there under the same set of circumstances, not knowing what to expect.

Q: The impression I got from them is that they didn't really know what they were there for. There were rumors.

Mr. Cooper: It was a rumor. It was strictly a rumor. We didn't know, as they said, until we got there. Well, we got there and we found out, "This is it. You're here for officer candidate training." Of course, at that time they called us "90-day wonders." So I anticipated, as they did, that we would simply go over to main side and start in officer candidate school. It developed, however, that they set up a separate school for us at Camp Robert Smalls.* Obviously, most of our instructors were white. Fortunately, at least one of us was already familiar with almost every subject we were exposed to. We decided early in the game that we were going to either sink or swim together. If we were going to swim, we were going to swim together; if we were going to sink, we were all going to sink together--even to the point of studying together in the head after lights out.

Here I am reminded of one of my favorite quotations:

---

*Within the Great Lakes Naval Training Station, Camp Robert Smalls was the site of training for black recruits. It was named for an escaped slave who captured the Confederate steamer Planter during the Civil War and turned her over to the U. S. Navy. He served as pilot of the Planter and later of the gunboat Keokuk.

"All that is needed for evil to flourish is that good men do nothing." While we didn't think of ourselves as "good" men, we knew to the man that if we failed in this endeavor the evil of segregation in the Navy, as related to black officers, would be set back for only God knows how long. We had to do <u>something</u>, and that something was to make it work!

Q: Did you get the feeling that the Navy was making a good-faith effort to get you to succeed?

Mr. Cooper: Yes and no. I think that the Navy as an institution was making a good-faith effort because it had been ordered to do so by the Commander in Chief. The "no" response relates to the fact that the institution is made up of people with their personal likes and dislikes. To that extent, they impact on the institution, and responses become institutionalized. I don't believe that the brass in Washington said, "Make these men fail." I think it was the result of what I would call institutional racism, and how individuals who served as our instructors, and who supervised our activities, felt in their hearts. I don't think that BuPers said, "Send them through the mill. Give 'em hell and flunk 'em."* I think it was more the institutionalized racism, which, incidentally, in my

---
*BuPers--Bureau of Naval Personnel.

judgment, is still alive and well in this country.

Q: Was John Dille an exception to that?*

Mr. Cooper: John was the best exception to the norm. We had some good instructors, two or three of them, but John was the exception and obviously has stuck with us ever since.

Q: What did he do for you?

Mr. Cooper: He went over and above the call of duty, beyond the subject matter that he was teaching and in charge of, to be an inspiration to us. John was perceptive enough to recognize what was going on. And again, I simply refuse to say that the Navy said, "Do this." Racism was just an accepted thing. I don't think they were doing it because of us personally; they would have done it to any group of potential black officers. And John knew and understood this and gave us a hell of a lot of support, and gave us support when we really needed it.

Q: In what ways?

---

*Lieutenant John F. Dille, Jr., USNR, was part of the group training the future black officers in 1944. He discusses his memories of that experience in his own oral history.

Mr. Cooper: In being understanding and helping us think through situations that arose in the course of that training. I don't know if the other fellows told you about it, but when our grades were sent to Washington, we came out two-tenths of a point above any indoctrination class that they'd ever had. They said, "It's a mistake. Send them back through." And we started the whole thing over again.

Q: Were you tested periodically?

Mr. Cooper: Yes. And again, we were serious about the business of sinking or swimming together, you know. I can remember sitting in those barracks and sitting in the head at night after lights out, just drilling each other back and forth until it literally hurt, because we were convinced that if one of us made it, we were all going to make it.

Q: It's ironic that you all didn't make it. There were three who didn't. I'm curious why Alves, Pinkney, and Williams did not make it.* Do you know why they were not

---
*Coxswain A. Alves; Yeoman Third Class J. B. Pinkney; Specialist Second Class Lewis R. Williams. Williams discusses his memories of the 1944 training experience in a Naval Institute oral history.

commissioned?

Mr. Cooper: Not those three, and there was another one who simply did not have enough to make it on.

Q: Native intelligence?

Mr. Cooper: Native intelligence. I think that was his problem, and he subsequently committed suicide, unfortunately.* I suspect in the other cases there were personality conflicts and difficulties that the guys were not able to overcome. And to a large extent, I can understand it, because we went through hell. I mean, we went through living hell.

Q: In what way?

Mr. Cooper: Just the sheer attitude of the people who were responsible for us.

Q: Was there overt hazing?

Mr. Cooper: Yes. You name it, and we had it. And again, I think that, as anything new, there were an awful lot of

―――――――
*This is a reference to Charles B. Lear, who was made a warrant boatswain at the conclusion of the training program. He was the only member of the Golden Thirteen who was not commissioned as an ensign.

people who simply didn't want to see this happen. We'll talk about that. That will come up naturally a little bit later in this story. And that was straight across the board--enlisted men, officers, petty officers, you name it, straight across the board. People simply didn't want to see it and were willing to do almost anything to keep it from happening, short of killing people.

Q: What sorts of things did they do? Were they fair in their testing of you?

Mr. Cooper: I think they had to be that. If they give a written test, you know how you respond. It's hard to fake. That's how come our grades were so good, and people resented that. I suspect that they knew that we had to be studying together, and they'd come around to check more than normal to see if lights were really out, for instance. Just little things like that. A million little things that are hard to describe but which you could see and feel almost immediately if you were in that situation. You just sense it and know what's going on. Of course, it takes a certain kind of determination to both accept that and respond to it creatively, which we had decided we were going to do, too. We were going to never give anybody, unless somebody said, "Well, I'm just going to blow your brains out," any reason to kick us out.

Well, anyway, I was called to main side one day, to Commander Armstrong's office.* I didn't know what he wanted, because at this point in time we were going back through the thing for the second time. It was in that time frame. In the course of that conversation, he said, "I don't know what kind of an officer you'd make for the Navy. In the first place, you're what we call a hell-raiser."

I said, "Sir, I don't recall having raised any hell since I've been here, and certainly not at Hampton when I was down there as a chief petty officer."

He said, "This goes back to when you were eight years old and the fight you had with a white boy in Washington, North Carolina."

Q: That had to be stretching pretty far.

Mr. Cooper: So I said, "Well, there's nothing I can say about that, sir. If you're aware of it, you must know the circumstances, and that's all I can say." What I didn't know was that he had my commission on his desk at that time.

---

*Commander Daniel W. Armstrong, USNR, was officer in charge of Camp Robert Smalls. A 1915 graduate of the Naval Academy, he resigned his regular commission in 1919 to pursue a civilian career. He was recalled to active duty for World War II, serving at Great Lakes and in the Pacific theater. Daniel Armstrong (1893-1947) was the son of Samuel Chapman Armstrong, founder of Hampton Institute. He was born the same year his father died.

So then in the course of 24 hours, as I remember, we all had our interviews and got our commissions. I was the only one of the group who could go into ship's stores and put on a uniform and walk out with it. Everybody else had to have it altered.

Q: Because of your size.

Mr. Cooper: Because of size. I was the first black man to wear a naval officer's uniform because my size was just right. I went in and walked out with it that day.

Fortunately, over that weekend we had liberty, and my wife was in Hamilton, Ohio, getting ready to have our baby. I was going home to see my family. I walked into the railroad station in Chicago, and that whole station stood still--literally. As I would walk through, everywhere I'd go, everything would stop.

Q: Double-take.

Mr. Cooper: And the same thing on the train. That was the beginning of a real experience.

Commander Downes had made arrangements for me to go back to Hampton, to the naval training school, and made me his personnel officer. Again, all of the trainees were black. The preponderance of ship's company was white, and obviously all of the officers except me were white. Again, you run into racism, as you see here at home. Many members of ship's company just simply refused to salute you. If they'd see you coming, they would cross the street and get on the other side of the street.

How do you deal with something like this? You can't go in to the skipper and say, "I want to resign." There's no such thing as resigning. So I developed a technique that if I ran into difficulty with you, and you were either an officer, petty officer, or ship's company, as personnel officer, I could develop something that would require us to be together. I did that time and time and time again, in the hope that as we sat down man to man to solve your problem, that you would recognize me as a human being.

Q: What were some examples of some of these things that you used as devices to get together with people?

Mr. Cooper: For instance, if a guy needed to go on emergency leave, he didn't have to come through the personnel office. I mean, that's just a routine thing. You just set it up so the guy goes. If his mother is dying, he's got to go home. He didn't have to talk to the personnel officer, but I made it so that he had to come through me to get that leave to go home. I'm sitting down talking to him about his mother who's dying, or he thinks his mother is dying, and he needs to go home and get there before she dies.

You start empathizing with this guy, and he begins to see you as a human being and not as a black son of a bitch with a shingle on his shoulder.* It would work almost invariably. In a situation like that, particularly in a training school, you could think up a thousand reasons to see somebody. A personnel problem could develop in the shop. A personnel problem developed out at Hampton Roads, which normally a chief would take care of. You just say, "Well, handle this, Chief." But you would bring it into your office. The technique worked time and time again.

Q: And presumably some of these people were spreading the word after they'd dealt with you.

Mr. Cooper: Exactly. There's a rippling effect. You see, I was the only black officer in a radius of 500 miles. My wife and daughter and I were walking down the street one day in Newport News, and a sailor got a foot away from my face. And he said, "You black son of a bitch, I read about you guys, but I never thought I'd meet one."

That's the one and only time I ever lost my cool. I really started after him. My wife grabbed my arm and said,

---
*"Shingle on his shoulder" refers to the shoulder boards on Cooper's uniform, denoting his rank as an officer.

"George, it's not worth it." But if she hadn't been there, I'd have been in trouble. That was the one time I lost my cool in the whole time I was in this situation.

I very quickly thought and said, "Peg, you're right. Thank you."

Q: Right. She helped you.

Mr. Cooper: I walked away from it. But that was the only time that I almost really got in trouble, because he was either going to beat me up, or I was going to beat him up at that moment in time.

Q: Was Downes supportive?

Mr. Cooper: Let me tell you a story which would document where he came from. I was officer of the day. I went in to pick up an officer who was coming in on assignment. I went to the airport and picked him up. He looked at me and said, "You obviously are assigned to the school."

I said, "Yes, sir." He was a captain.

He said, "Well, where am I going to stay tonight?"

I said, "You're going to stay in the BOQ."*

He said, "Where do you stay?"

I said, "I live in an apartment, sir."

---

*BOQ--bachelor officers' quarters.

He said, "Good. But before I go to bed, I want to see the skipper."

I said, "Sir, you can't see the skipper tonight. You can see the skipper at quarters tomorrow, because I'm not going to call him tonight."

He said, "Well, I've got a problem."

I said, "Can I help you with the problem?"

He said, "You are the problem."

I said, "There's nothing I can do about it then. I'm sure that I'm not going to call the skipper tonight, and you'll have to, sir, see him at quarters the next morning." I took him to the BOQ and put him up for the night.

Well, all of us had to go to quarters the next morning. This guy got there early. Commander Downes was the kind of guy who always got to work 45 minutes, an hour before time. He was always in his office. So when I got there, this officer had, in fact, already seen the skipper and gone.

So we went in to quarters, and the captain said, "We had a new officer come in last night. George met him, and he came in this morning early to see me. He told me that if he had known there was a colored officer on this base, he would have asked not to be sent here, because he never wanted to see another nigger as long as he lived." Downes said, "I've been in touch with BuPers, and he won't stay here. We're going to ship him out. He's going to Alaska."

He didn't come in. I never saw him anymore. The skipper came to quarters three weeks later and said, "You remember that captain who came in here and said he never wanted to see a 'nigger'? We sent him up to Alaska and he never saw one, because he died yesterday."

Q: Do you remember his name?

Mr. Cooper: No. But I will never forget that story. I'm sure in my own mind that Downes had a lot to do with my being one of the members of Golden Thirteen. He had to have done that.

Q: What qualities do you think led to your being picked for that group?

Mr. Cooper: That's really a $64,000 question. I don't know. I honestly don't know.

Q: I've been looking into the backgrounds, and they were fairly diverse, from different geographical areas, different levels of education, different social strata. It seemed almost as if you were a laboratory group, and they wanted to introduce several variables to see what effect it would have.

Mr. Cooper: I'm sure that was the case. I'm sure that was the case. But what specifically got me into the group, I'll never know. I just simply don't know. By this time, I'd worked with Commander Downes for better than two years, and we'd really gotten to be good friends.

One of the things that the skipper used to win friends and influence people was the metal shop. We had a Class A training school, and in the metalsmith shop we had a guy who was a whiz at metal spinning, and we set up a lathe so he could spin. The skipper would have him make things for people in Washington, so that when he went to Washington, he would drop something on an officer's desk, and whatever he wanted, he walked out with it.

The man who did this for us was Joe Gilliard. He worked at Hampton Institute in the art department. I'm sure he has retired by now, but he was a real craftsman, and metal spinning was one of his fortes. He used to spin some of the most gorgeous pieces you've ever seen in your life, primarily out of copper and brass for the skipper.

Q: What sorts of things did he make?

Mr. Cooper: Candlesticks, lamps, that kind of thing. We used to make miniature coal scuttles. You know what a coal scuttle is?

Q: It's a bucket, essentially.

Mr. Cooper: It's a bucket that you put coal in and sit it next to the fireplace. If you're burning coal in the fireplace, you put it in there. Or you use a coal scuttle to put coal in a furnace. We used to make miniature ones out of brass. They were quite attractive little gadgets, and he used to use these as gifts, too. But he knew how to win friends and influence people, and he knew how to play whatever game needed to be played to get what he wanted done accomplished. I'm sure it was through him that I got to be in this group, because I don't think there was anything I had done particularly.

Q: You were officially the personnel officer. I have a feeling you took more than an ordinary interest in the metalsmith operation.

Mr. Cooper: Oh, yes. Yes, because that obviously was still going on but no longer a part of my responsibility and duties at the base.

So then I was finally ordered overseas--to the South Pacific. But before I say that, let me go back to when we were in training at Great Lakes. They had this contraption built up over the swimming pool to teach you how to abandon ship. You've probably been there. You go up and jump off this thing into the pool. Well, some joker had left a bar of soap up there, and I stepped on this bar of soap and fell in the pool and hurt my back. I was in and out of hospitals for out-patient treatment, never went in for in-patient treatment of this back injury. They wanted to operate, but I wouldn't consent to it. I'd fake it and say, "I'm all right," and go back to duty.

But finally, I was ordered to the South Pacific and went to Norfolk and got the first real examination I'd had since I'd been in the Navy. They discovered this back injury and said, "We can't send you out. You've got to go." So I got a medical discharge, and that's how I got out of the Navy.

Q: What year was that?

Mr. Cooper: Nineteen forty-five, before the end of the war.

Q: Did you get the feeling that someone had deliberately left the soap there to sabotage the thing?

Mr. Cooper: No, I don't think so. That thought never crossed my mind.

Cooper #1 - 37

Q: I can't imagine why anybody would take a bar of soap up there.

Mr. Cooper: I can't either, but I never thought that anybody did it deliberately, because, in the first place, who's going to know who's going to go up there next? I don't think it was deliberate. I think it was just accidental, one of those things. Then I got my discharge from the service and went back to Hampton to start a veterans' program, because people were coming back then, out of service, being discharged from World War II, and colleges and universities were starting veterans' programs. I went back and did that, and then subsequently became the director of the trade school from which I had graduated.

Q: Were you disappointed that you did not get shipboard duty?

Mr. Cooper: Not really. Not really. I enjoyed my work at the school. I really liked it. I had a young family and was not really that anxious to leave them, you know. And this was a way of serving and having your cake and eating it, too. I felt that I was doing a good job in the billet that I was in. My ratings indicated that. So I had no qualms about going overseas at all, or going aboard ship, for sea duty. I suppose I was never cut out, really, to be in the service. I always had problems with somebody telling me when I needed to go where: "You don't need to stay here any longer; you need to go over here." And you have no choice in the matter--you go. I had real problems with that.

Q: Understandably, since you'd been facing that kind of situation for years.

Mr. Cooper: So that I didn't have any qualms about sea duty or overseas duty or whatever.

Q: I'd just like to run through the names of your fellow students to see what recollections you have of them as individuals while you were undergoing the training. What do you remember of Jesse Arbor, for example?*

Mr. Cooper: Loudmouth, hale, hearty sort of guy. Didn't give a damn about much of anything, the salt of the earth, would do anything for you, simply because he knows you. A hell of a nice guy. I think Jesse's forte was identification. He helped us more than anything else in terms of aircraft identification, and he seemingly had a gift in that regard. I told you one of us knew something

---

*Jesse W. Arbor is a member of the Golden Thirteen. He discusses his recollections in his own Naval Institute oral history.

about most of the subject matters that we had to deal with.

Q: I gather he was also good at keeping your spirits up.

Mr. Cooper: Oh, yes. Jesse always has a joke. He lived it. If he felt that things were getting down, he'd come up with something, and he didn't have to reach for it, you know; it was right there on the tip of his tongue. He played a substantial role in keeping our morale up. Again, that was just Jesse's forte. He's still that way.

Q: He said he thought he was picked for the group because he had two main assets: "runnin' my mouth and bossin' like hell."

Mr. Cooper: Pretty good. That's pretty good, yes. He's quite a guy.

Q: How about Phillip Barnes?*

Mr. Cooper: Phil Barnes was very quiet. Not the easiest man in the world to get to know, but once you got to know Phil, you really appreciated him as a decent, sincere, hard-working individual. He was fat, and he felt that. I

---

*Phillip G. Barnes was a member of the Golden Thirteen. He died before he could be interviewed by the Naval Institute.

Cooper #1 - 40

don't know whether you would call it some sort of an inferiority complex, but he knew he was fat.

Q: He was self-conscious about it.

Mr. Cooper: He was self-conscious about it, and I think that had something to do with his being not as forward as some of the rest of us were. But an awfully nice guy, and we got along famously. Not just he and I, but all of us with him.

Q: I think he had a sister who was in Washington that could give you some information, unofficially, on what was going on.

Mr. Cooper: Yes. You did interview some people, didn't you? Yes. That was not too bad a deal, you know. That helped tremendously, too. And he knew exactly how to handle that so that neither he nor his sister nor anybody else got in trouble. But for that and some other reasons, he was a real influence on the group.

Q: How about Sam Barnes?*

---

*Samuel E. Barnes is a member of the Golden Thirteen. He discusses his recollections in his own Naval Institute oral history.

Mr. Cooper: Sam was the typical athlete-coach kind of guy--just another one of the guys, a regular fellow. He was not just a member of the group--he helped keep it alive, as he is still doing today. I suppose in terms of average, as it relates to being pushy, he would be a little below average in terms of being outward like Dennis Nelson, for instance, or like Goodwin, but a hell of a nice guy and definitely an important part of the group.*

Q: Dalton Baugh.**

Mr. Cooper: A leader, very open, very outgoing, very forward, matter of fact. As an engineer, he had that down-to-earth kind of approach to things, which was very helpful, too, because we were in some critical times then and some critical situations. He was matter of fact: "What's the situation here? Let's look at it."

Q: "Let's analyze it."

Mr. Cooper: "Let's analyze it." A practical point of view. That precisely is what Dalton brought to the group, I think, supported by my approach to things, because I was pretty much that way, too.

---
*Dennis D. Nelson II and Reginald E. Goodwin were members of the Golden Thirteen. Both died before they could be interviewed by the Naval Institute.
**Dalton L. Baugh was a member of the Golden Thirteen. He died before he could be interviewed by the Naval Institute.

Q: I'm wondering--and this is really a rhetorical question--whether this diversity of talents that you brought was a deliberate thing on the part of the Navy or just an accidental happenstance, that each of you was an expert in a certain aspect of things.

Mr. Cooper: I don't know how the Navy could have known that. Our background checks certainly would have indicated the diversity in terms of background, generally, so that that was probably deliberate in an effort to get a true cross-section. I think they got a pretty good cross-section. Beyond that, I'm not sure.

Q: For examples, Alves, I guess, had merchant seaman experience.

Mr. Cooper: Yes, and he was the only one who had had that.

Q: Reginald Goodwin.

Mr. Cooper: Very reserved. I started to say "typical attorney," but I'm not sure that that's fair. Very reserved, obviously very bright, and he was a bright young man and was a bright man, obviously, the rest of his life. Had been at Great Lakes for some time prior to this experience, therefore knew the ropes there in a pretty good fashion.

Q: I gather he was used as a go-between to main side, to Armstrong.

Mr. Cooper: And played that role very well, I'm sure to the satisfaction of the skipper.

Q: It was useful for the rest of you to have somebody in that role also, wasn't it?

Mr. Cooper: Oh, yes. Again, this was because we decided, as a group, that we were going to work as a group, and that whatever I knew that would be helpful to that group, I was going to come forth with it, no matter where it came from or under what circumstances I got it. If it was going to be helpful to us as a group, it was laid on the table. And Goodwin was a part of the group.

Q: James Hair.

Mr. Cooper: Hair was very talkative, but in a different kind of a way than Arbor, in a different kind of a way than Baugh. I suspect he leaned more toward intellectualizing than any of the rest of us, but even in that light, had a role to play in this scenario. Incidentally, he's still playing that same role.

Q: What is the role?

Mr. Cooper: I don't know. It's hard as hell to put your finger on it, but it's there. Hair has a knack for getting things done that's a little uncanny. This relates itself to his ability to deal with people in a very, in my judgment, unusual kind of way. He has something about him which tends to disarm people so that they trust him immediately. And a lot of us have difficulty in that area, in gaining trust right off the bat. But Hair has some sort of quality that just simply disarms people, and you start unburdening yourself to him right away.

He also has a way of responding to that, which I think is a little unusual, and he responds to it in a fashion that makes you believe that you're coming out with the answers instead of him coming out with them. The more you know him, the more you get to know that Hair is doing this deliberately, and you can see him playing this game. It's a hell of a good game to play.

Q: It's good psychology.

Mr. Cooper: Because it makes you feel so much better as a

human being. It's a quality that I wish I had. He's quite a guy.

Q: What role did he play in your group as you were studying together?

Mr. Cooper: Again, helping us intellectualize situations that arose and how to best deal with them. That's what I remember most about him. He was a pretty good student; I remember that.

Q: You all must have been.

Mr. Cooper: But in helping us analyze how to proceed and respond to various issues and situations that arose, I think he was very helpful.

Q: Charles Lear.

Mr. Cooper: Lear was what might be described as a hard-nosed chief petty officer. I'm not sure that that was the best thing for this group, but at the same time, it may be that the group needed some of that to help it go through some of the things that it went through, if I'm making any kind of sense at all. Very lovable, but very much the chief petty officer type guy, if that makes sense to you.

Q: Was he in fact a chief petty officer?

Mr. Cooper: No, but he was as close to it as you could get in terms of how he responded to things, in his perception of what the appropriate response would be.

Q: Was he the sort who would prod if it was called for?

Mr. Cooper: I don't think so, particularly. If this is the way it is, this is the way it is, so let's do it that way. I think that's probably what I'm alluding to when I say "sort of a chief petty officer kind of guy." "These are the regulations. Let's go. Don't raise too much question about it. If it's what the book says to do, let's do it." But again, we, time after time, I suspect, needed that kind of influence, too, because we were in a peculiar situation. We were in the kind of situation I'm not sure anybody can really understand unless he was there, truly, really understand. You just had to be there to appreciate it fully.

Q: I'm trying to use this medium so that all the rest of us who weren't there can try to understand it.

Cooper #1 - 47

Graham Martin.*

Mr. Cooper: Strictly a football coach. He was the coach, and that's about all you can say about Graham, but that's saying a hell of a lot about him. His approach was, "If you are going to be on this team, you've got to make the grade. You've got to make the grade on classroom work; you've got to make the grade out here in the field; you've got to make the grade, period, if you're going to be on this team." And he brought that to that group, too. If you were going to be on this team, you were going to have to bring it intellectually, you have to bring it physically, you have to bring it spiritually, every kind of way that needs to be brought, you're going to bring it. That was his background, and that's what he brought to the group, much to our advantage. Much to our advantage.

Q: The thing he takes great pride in is the ability to inspire.

Mr. Cooper: Yes. And that's what he did as a coach, and that's what he did with the Golden Thirteen. I mean, he was right there. That was his job, and he did it. Again, there was time after time after time when we'd be down in the dumps and Graham would come back with, "Oh, no, man.

---
*Graham E. Martin is a member of the Golden Thirteen. He discusses his recollections in his own Naval Institute oral history.

Let's get our crap together here." You never forget any of those guys, obviously.

Q: He said his wife wanted him to stay in the Navy, but he never wanted to be anything but a coach, and that was his life's work.

Mr. Cooper: That's right.

Q: Dennis Nelson.

Mr. Cooper: Dennis was the playboy, smart. I mean, bright. Dennis was really a bright man, knew what he wanted, knew pretty much what he was going to do to get what he wanted and how he was going to get there. Not conceited, but leaning in that direction. Quite a showman. I suppose Dennis had every kind of a naval officer's uniform there ever was made, and he enjoyed this.

Q: Including a cape.

Mr. Cooper: Including a cape, no less. But interestingly enough, Dennis looked good in all of it.

Q: And took great pride in that.

Mr. Cooper: And took great pride in it, yes, and used it to his advantage and, I suspect, to the advantage of the service.

Q: Was he brash?

Mr. Cooper: Yes.

Q: Was he too brash?

Mr. Cooper: From our perspective, yes, but obviously not from his, and maybe not from a lot of other people's perspective. I thought so. Some other people thought so, but who the hell were we to judge? If it hadn't been for Dennis, we'd have never gotten back together, for instance, as the Golden Thirteen. I mean, he was singularly responsible for that.

Q: Was he the one who coined the name Golden Thirteen?

Mr. Cooper: As far as I know, he came up with it, yes. Dennis worked on this. He didn't just work on it six months; Dennis worked on this for two or three years to try to get us back together as a group. We owe him a lot.

Cooper #1 - 50

Q: I've talked to Admiral Gravely, and he wound up achieving a number of the firsts that Dennis Nelson might have.* I'm wondering if perhaps Nelson's personality worked against him after a certain point.

Mr. Cooper: I would not be surprised, because, as you say, Sam made it. You didn't know Dennis, but you know Sam. Dennis was almost the opposite, you know. Understanding how Sam would have made it, you can understand why Dennis would not have made it just from talking to people who knew him. He was a nice guy, lovable. You had to love him. My wife was crazy about him. Everybody was crazy about him.

Q: He probably could rub some people the wrong way.

Mr. Cooper: He had a knack for doing that, rubbing some people the wrong way. But it takes all kinds to make a world.

Q: John Reagan.**

Mr. Cooper: John's the salt of the earth, quiet, very unassuming, but, in my judgment, very profound. Quite a

---
*Vice Admiral Samuel L. Gravely, Jr., USN, (Ret.) was the first black officer selected for flag rank in the U. S. Navy. He has been interviewed as part of the Naval Institute's oral history program.
**John W. Reagan is a member of the Golden Thirteen. He discusses his recollections in his own oral history.

gentleman, always the gentleman.

Q: What did he bring to the group?

Mr. Cooper: I suspect a sense of serenity, if that makes any sense to you. I see him playing that role even today as we get back together. There is a light side to him, which is a joy to behold, but beyond that, and more importantly, a serious side to him, which one has to respect and admire. I think that John has it like no other member of the group has that. I just enjoy being around him--more for that reason, I think, than for any other.

Q: Do you have any examples of his light side? Would it be a more refined, more subtle type of humor than Arbor's?

Mr. Cooper: Yes, yes. Oh, Lord, yes. There's no question. Far removed from the kind of humor that you think of when you think about Arbor. Very subtle, but there. You very clearly see it. Some people don't, but it's there.

Q: Would you describe him as witty?

Mr. Cooper: Probably. Probably, but with the wit, a

seriousness that overshadows the wit, so that you know that here's a witty man who knows he's being witty and knows when to be witty, and who also knows that there's a more serious side to everything we are about, and that we'd damn well better get with that serious side pretty quickly, if that makes any sense to you. It does to me. And that's John Reagan, as I see him. For instance, the Golden Thirteen had some stationery printed up, and John wrote to each of us and said, "I wish you would do me a favor. I wish you would write me a letter on this stationery in your handwriting, just for my files." There isn't another member of the Golden Thirteen who would have thought of that but John Reagan. And that means a hell of a lot to John.

Q: Frank Sublett.

Mr. Cooper: Frank came with a mechanical background, and based on that mechanical background, was able to be helpful in a lot of the stuff that we were about in training. A very decent human being. In fact, I think all the guys were decent human beings.

Q: He also strikes me as very friendly.

Mr. Cooper: Oh, yes. You love Frank as soon as you meet

him; he's just like my puppy out there. You just love him from the get-go. Very friendly, very open kind of guy, meets people very easily, makes you feel comfortable immediately upon meeting him. He's a very straightforward kind of happy-go-lucky guy. I enjoy him tremendously, him and his wife.

Q: Syl White.*

Mr. Cooper: The judge. Obviously an intellectual of the last order.

Q: Also a proud man.

Mr. Cooper: Very proud, and is never going to let anybody forget that there's a serious side to everything. That's not all bad, not by a long shot. Expresses himself well, thinks deeply, in my judgment, and is a pretty profound guy.

Q: The kinds of people who get the job that he has are profound guys.

Mr. Cooper: Yes, yes, yes. He wears it, in my judgment,

---
*William Sylvester White is a member of the Golden Thirteen. He discusses his recollections in his own Naval Institute oral history.

Cooper #1 - 54

well. You know, I've seen just innumerable people who get positions of esteem, prestige, authority, and it goes immediately to their heads.

Q: George Cooper. What did you bring to the group?

Mr. Cooper: Nothing.

Q: I don't believe that.

Mr. Cooper: I just happened to be there. I was pretty good in math and was helpful in that area as we were in school. I think I like people. That's been my work all my life, working with people, and maybe had some influence on keeping us together. I suspect my ability to work with people, to facilitate--added to Baugh's analytical approach--helped us stay together.

Q: You described the process of getting out of the Navy and working with the veterans. How long did that last?

Mr. Cooper: A year and a half. Then they asked me if I would take over as director of the Department of Trade Training at Hampton, which was the old Trade School. So I went into that and took that over and worked at that for about four years. My wife's home is in Hamilton, Ohio, which is 35 miles south of Dayton.

Q: How did you happen to meet her? We didn't cover that. I'm a little curious.

Mr. Cooper: We met at Hampton Institute. I did my undergraduate work at Hampton before going on to Columbia to get a master's in personnel administration and then started on a doctorate at Ohio State. We met at Hampton. My senior year at Hampton, she came as a library student. Hampton had one of the best schools of library science in the country. And she came to Hampton, having gone to school here at Central State, to do graduate work in library science, and that's how we got to know each other. We met on the football field. At the end of that school year, at Christmastime, we got married. I think we knew right away that this was what each of us wanted, because it was not a long courtship.

Q: She had some ties with Ohio, and you had certainly been here before, too.

Mr. Cooper: After we were married, we shared a keen interest in the theater. We'd come to visit her parents and her family in Hamilton, but we would always arrange to do it at the time when "Shakespeare under the stars" was at

Antioch College over here in Yellow Springs, just 12 miles from here. We'd plan our trips so we'd stop in Dayton to check out the outdoor theater, Shakespeare, and then, at the same time, visit with her family in Hamilton.

In the course of doing that, I became very friendly with a family in Dayton, Cal and Evelyn Crawford. My wife and they had been in school together at Wilberforce. We'd come by and we'd see them. This guy Cal Crawford was in the house-cleaning business, which I had never heard of. We got to talking about it, and I said, "Cal, why don't I go to work with you one day? I want to see what the hell you do. I mean, what do you really do when you clean a house?"

So he said, "Fine. Get up in the morning, and let's go to work." So I got up the next morning and put on one of his gray uniforms. The name of his company was Finer Services, Incorporated. I got in the truck and went to work with Cal and his crew. They walked into a house similar to this one, washed down all the walls, cleaned all the carpets, the overstuffed furniture, the hardwood floors, out in one day. Windows, the whole works, or as much of that as you wanted done.

So when we got back that evening, we were sitting at the dinner table, and he said, "What do you think of my business?"

I said, "I think it's a good business, but I would

never let you in my house a second time."

He said, "What?"

I said, "You had more stuff scattered around in that house, I was wondering how the hell we were ever going to get it out. It's just tacky."

He said, "What do you think I ought to do?"

I said, "I think you ought to package the thing, and if you package it right, you've got something to sell, and you could make a fortune off of it."

He said, "Well, if you're so damn smart, why don't you come here and help me package it?" And he was serious.

So I toyed with the idea, and it was about time then for me to get a sabbatical from Hampton. So I took a half-year's leave of absence and I said, "I'll come out here and work with you. I'll help you set this damn thing up. We'll put it in a package and make it salable."

Q: Was this about 1950?

Mr. Cooper: Yes, in 1952. So I came out here for a half year. That's what I intended to come out for. We put this package together. We packaged this thing and made it look like a professional operation, because it was really good.

Q: What do you mean by packaging?

Mr. Cooper: Well, Cal was lazy, and he wasn't washing the walls out of a bucket. He had a compressor hooked up, so he would spray the cleaning solution on the wall and take the dirt off with a sponge. The compressor was here, and the motor was there. I just said, "Let's put it in a little case and make it look like a machine." It was, in fact, a machine, but it just looked like the devil.

In the course of that six-month period, there was a fire in Rike's Department Store, the major department store in downtown Dayton. I was coming home from church and heard about this fire and drove down there. I heard about this fire down at Rike's on the radio, coming home from church, so I went down there. I started in, and this big-bellied cop said, "You can't go in there."

I said, "These people need me." I showed him a card that said smoke damage specialist.

He said, "I suspect they do. You better go in."

Q: How did you happen to have such a card?

Mr. Cooper: During this period, I had written a manual for house cleaning. We were on the radio. We had radio spots and newspaper advertising.

Q: And that was one of the things that you did?

Mr. Cooper: That was one of the things we did, was smoke damage specialists. We'd go in after a fire and clean it up. So I went in and showed this card to a secretary, I suppose. I don't know how all these people got down there so fast, but Rike himself was there. So I got in to see him. He said, "We need you to put us back in business."

I said, "I think we can put you back in business tomorrow if the whole store didn't burn down."

He said, "How many people can you get to come in?"

I said, "I suspect I can get two dozen to come in right away within the hour." We put them back in business the next day. And our business started jumping.

Then I got sick. I came down with spinal meningitis. So the doctor said, "You're going to either have a short leg or a twisted back or something's going to happen to you. You can expect that, number one. Number two, I don't know what you're doing for a living, but whatever you're doing, you ought to get out of it. Do something with a little less stress." Crawford was a genius, but he was lazy, and I was literally trying to hold that business together and make it develop into something. We had even developed franchises. We started in Hamilton and intended going out from there across the state of Ohio.

So I came home and I was telling Peg about it that evening. Looking at the paper, I saw an ad for a housing inspector for the city of Dayton. In the meantime, I'd started building a house here, because I had decided to stay here. I was just going to quit Hampton despite the tenure. I was tired of the academic world and I needed something a little different, so I decided to stay in Dayton.

I went downtown and took an examination. A couple of weeks later, I came back and discovered that I had come out on top, and they offered me this job as a housing inspector. It was a natural for me because of my background at Hampton, where I had at least a speaking knowledge of all the building trades. I was offered the job at $96.00 a week. So I said to Crawford, "Crawford, I think I'd better take this job."

He said, "George, you can't afford to take this job. You know how much money we're making, and you're going to take a job for $96.00 a week, and you just built a house?"

I said, "Well, my wife is working." She was in the library. I said, "Peg's working, and I think my health is more important. The doctor told me that I should get out of this, so I'm going to quit." So I did. I quit and took this job with the city as housing inspector. That job lasted a year, until I was offered a job in city planning. I've always been very active civically; it's just a part of me. Wherever I go, I like to get involved in the community to the extent possible.

I was riding on the elevator one day with Robert

Flynn, the director of planning for the city. He said, "George, how would you like to work for me?"

I said, "Bob, I don't even know how to spell planning. I'm not a planner."

He said, "We need the kind of expertise that I've seen come from you as you work with community groups. We need that input into the planning process. The problem is that if you come to work for me, I can't offer you any more money, but in a year I can give you a decent salary."

I said, "Okay, let's take a shot at it." So I did that and went into planning. I worked there for about six or seven years.

One of the things I like to remember from that time related to having instituted The Dayton Fund for Home Rehabilitation. This nonprofit entity--still in existence and now a public charity--makes grants and low-interest loans to disadvantaged homeowners who don't meet the means test for loans from a financial institution. Some repayment schedules are as low as $5.00 per month.

Q: Does that bring you up to about 1960?

Mr. Cooper: Yes.

While I was at Hampton, in the trade school, I developed a co-op program where we would send the kids from the trade school out in the industry to work for a quarter and then come back to school. I also helped develop an exchange program between Hampton and Antioch College. (Antioch started the co-op concept in education.)

So Edward Miller, with whom I'd worked over there in this exchange student program between Hampton and Antioch, called me one day and said, "George, why don't you come over. The president wants to talk to you." That was at Antioch. I was living in Dayton, obviously, working for the city as a senior planner. We had lived on a college campus obviously at Hampton since I was there in the Navy and as a faculty member at the college after the Navy.

What they wanted me to do sounded challenging, because I felt that Antioch was one of the few colleges in the country really serious about both general education and on-hands experiential education. Initially, I worked in what they called the extramural department, placing students in co-op jobs during their work quarters. I subsequently became the director of Antioch's international work-study program, which necessitated a good deal of foreign travel on an expense account. That's how we got to see half of the world, because then you could take a hostess along, and my wife was obviously my hostess.

We would bring people in--businessmen, teachers, and engineers--from various parts of the world, keep them on campus for 90 days of indoctrination, and then put them out somewhere in the country to work from 18 to 24 months at their profession or business. Then ostensibly they went back home. Many of them never got back home because of how well they did here. I worked at that for about seven years.

Then I got a call from the city manager at Dayton. He said, "George, come over. I want to talk with you." His name is Jim Kunde.* Jim I had known when I was with the city as a planner. He was a student intern in the city manager's office. He was at this point in time, however, the city manager. So Jim called me in, and I went over to see him. He said, "It's time for me to appoint some black department directors. I'd like for you to be the first one."

I said, "Jim, what do you want me to do?"

He said, "Well, I've got three departments, and you can take any one of them." So we talked about it, and I decided that I would accept his offer to become his director of the Department of Human Resources, which took in corrections, housing, health, consumer protection, parks, recreation--about 900 people in seven divisions. So I accepted that job and worked at it until my retirement some five years ago. Again, I was the first black director in the city of Dayton. Since then five out of 14 directors have been black.

I retired and decided that I wanted to do something

---
*James E. Kunde was city manager of Dayton, Ohio, from February 1970 to September 1973.

about getting blacks into the mainstream of American business and industry. I believe the only way you're going to do that is to produce something, to make something, to provide opportunity for employment. I thought about it a good deal. Twenty years ago, if you needed an energy engineer, you'd have difficulty finding one, because there weren't that many around. Today I know six good black energy engineers. As I got thinking about that, it occurred to me that in almost any skill that you needed now, you could find it in the minority community pretty well developed, having developed over the past quarter of a century.

It occurred to me that if we, as a race, did not take advantage of that, we'd be missing the boat. It takes a little doing, but I discovered that you can find any kind of skill you want in the minority community. I'm hopeful that before the end of that lease that you just saw me sign today, that's five years from now, that we will have that big building that I showed you filled with people doing all kinds of fascinating things. I described one of them to you as it related to phosphorescent inks and paints and electroluminescent light panels. My wife said, "I thought we retired to see the world." I have an obligation to do some of that, too, and I think I can strike a happy balance and do some of both.

Q: There's a great sense of satisfaction from making that kind of a contribution.

Mr. Cooper: I think so. I think so. You know, I'm not sure whether it's going to be any significant contribution or not, but at least I'm going to give it a shot.

Q: Maybe you could put on this record some of the things you told me before we turned the tape on, of how you envision this thing working, that you're taking an old school building and going to use it as a day-care center and a manufacturing plant.

Mr. Cooper: Yes. The school is located just diagonally across from one of five General Motors plants in Dayton. It's one of the largest GM plants in Dayton; they hire a tremendously large complement of people. I think I can work with them in setting up day-care facilities to service their employees, plus the neighborhood. It's in a predominantly black neighborhood. I think Inland will support that. Inland is a division of General Motors, the name of this plant. So we will use one floor of a whole wing of this big school for that purpose. We're working with the Community Action Agency and the state in order to set this up. Hopefully, they will provide funding for it.

In this instance we are not only doing day care, but we're training paraprofessionals for the day-care industry. And there is a very severe shortage of people in that line of work now, which simply leads me to say that everything that we do in this school building is going to have a training component connected with it. We're going to use that not only to produce some things and to develop some minority businesses, but to train in-school youth working with the Dayton Board of Education and out-of-school youth working with the Dayton Urban League and the Community Action Agency. Each of these three entities has indicated a very sincere interest in this approach and in cooperating to make this thing possible.

We made preliminary contacts with a number of industries in the area, and they are interested in giving us subcontract work to help in this regard, and some of the things that we are manufacturing, some of the research and development contracts that we propose to get from Wright-Patterson Air Force Base, which is just adjacent to Dayton, will help us even to give some on-hands experience for youngsters who are interested in scientific fields. There's a lot of know-how in the Miami Valley, again, know-how that you couldn't find 20 years ago, but it's there now. We've started already pulling some of this know-how together to impact on this thing that we're about in this school. It's really kind of fascinating; at least I think so.

Q: What is your role in it?

Mr. Cooper: I perceive myself as simply being an expediter.

Q: You must have some standing in it to sign the lease on behalf of the group.

Mr. Cooper: I serve as the president. I started the company, really, and I brought in with me at this point the only other real partner in the business. We're in the process of setting it up now and involving a lot of other people. A guy who was in the subcontracting business in a little town south of Xenia, in Jamestown, where he simply outgrew his plant, and he's coming in with me and bringing his stuff with me, his work and his equipment, to help start us off. Then we were able to pick up about a half a million dollars worth of equipment from Monsanto Chemical, the plant that they were decommissioning. So we've got pretty close to three-quarters of a million dollars' worth of equipment to put in the school right away.

Q: Is it your goal to have this self-supporting or turn a profit by five years?

Mr. Cooper: Yes, turn a profit.

Q: What will you do with that money when it comes in? Is that going to be plowed back into the operation?

Mr. Cooper: I see it going back into the operation, because I'd like to see Community Industries, Inc., become a real force in American business and industry. The only way you can do that is if you make any money, to put it back in and make it bigger and better. I suspect that if I'm successful in simply getting this thing off the ground, it'll be worth the effort.

Q: And you can serve as an example for others to do the same thing.

Mr. Cooper: It would be worth the effort, yes. And another reason that I think the thing will work is that Dayton is the kind of community, unlike, in my perception, other communities across the country, that will grab onto an idea like this and help you make it work. The leadership in the Miami Valley is, in my judgment, very unusual. And when I say leadership, I'm talking about the leadership in business and industry, in terms of doing innovative and exciting things. I've seen it happen in many areas, and obviously this came as a result of my exposure with the city and with Antioch College.

Q: You've described a life of doing innovative things, service to others. Where does the Navy experience fit in the overall context of your life?

Mr. Cooper: I think it's a real cog. Since Dennis Nelson was instrumental in having the Navy get us back together on an annual basis, most of the time we have met with NNOA at the same time that they meet and in the same headquarters or hotel.* When you go into one of those meetings and walk in and see 400 and 500 good-looking, obviously bright, up-and-coming naval officers, and recognize that at least you had a part, played a little part in making this possible by being one of the first black officers and going through some of the things that we went through to make it work, that it was without question worthwhile to do it. You walk into one of those general sessions where all these young bright people are gathered together, the buttons just pop off your shirt, you're so proud of them.

There is a lot of compensation from the fact that you might have played a part in making this become a reality. In addition to that, you come to recognize that while, in my judgment, at least, institutional racism is still alive

---
*NNOA--National Naval Officers Association, an organization of black U. S. naval officers.

and well in America, the Navy--and, I suspect, the services--have come a long way in trying to address that. The door is open now both in the service and out of the service, and probably a little bit more in the service than out. Anybody now can go in and do pretty much what he's capable of doing, and become pretty much what he's capable of becoming. That was not the case when the Golden Thirteen went to Great Lakes.

I suspect that one way to say it is that I'm egotistical enough to believe that we had something to do with that by virtue of the way we responded to it, because if we had screwed that thing up, it would have been screwed up for a long, long time after that. We determined that we would not, in fact, screw it up, but we would make the best of it, and to the extent possible, make it work, from our end, anyway. So that I perceive of the short period of time that I spent in the Navy as having again made a contribution to something worthwhile.

Q: I can contemplate a scenario in which you had been competitive, instead of cooperative, and worked against each other, for example.

Mr. Cooper: Oh, yes, it could have very easily happened.

Q: Had that been the case, the group might not have succeeded. And this would have been ammunition for those who would say, "Negroes can't make it."

Mr. Cooper: And we were aware of that. That was a part of what kept us together and kept us approaching it from the perspective that we did approach it from.

Q: It's interesting that you've got much more celebrity in retrospect than you had at the time.

Mr. Cooper: I don't know.

Q: There was virtually no publicity of the fact that you were the first when you got your commissions, was there?

Mr. Cooper: Well . . .

Q: The Navy certainly wasn't putting it on billboards as a sign of social progress.

Mr. Cooper: Oh, no, no, no. I think the only thing nationally that was done was that we got our picture in Life magazine.* That was the only thing that I can think of that was done nationally in terms of the media. I think

---

*"First Negro Ensigns," Life, 24 April 1944, page 44.

Cooper #1 - 72

we made a contribution when we went aboard the Kidd, because there were two helicopters of media people that left out of Norfolk to join us on the Kidd.*

Q: That was in 1982.

Mr. Cooper: Yes. The free publicity that the Navy got out of that thing would just make your hair stand on edge. Again, you were part of something that helped the service along. And in terms of responses and reactions from the black community, we'll never be able to measure what that meant in terms of the reaction of that community, and that's one of the roles that we're still playing.

We're going into schools, and we're talking to young people whose parents still perceive of the Navy as an entity where the only thing you can do is be a steward's mate, and who are simply not aware of today's opportunities, particularly in an area like this, where you don't even see a sailor except in the recruiting command. A lot of that still exists in the minority community, and it's simply no longer the fact. To the extent that we can help overcome the steward's mate syndrome, we're still performing something of a service, in my judgment.

---

*From 13 to 15 April 1982, the nine surviving members of the Golden Thirteen held a reunion on board the guided missile destroyer Kidd (DDG-993) at sea in the Atlantic. See PH2 Drake White, "Golden 13 Together Again," All Hands, August 1982, pages 8-11.

Q: Judge White said that at the end of World War II, he got a letter from a black sailor in the Pacific who said that the Navy at that time was more democratic than the society it served, and the judge feels that is still true today.

Mr. Cooper: I think that's valid today, very valid today.

Q: You and the other members of the Golden Thirteen played a big part in that, so I'm grateful to you for spending this time to help document your achievement in that regard.

Mr. Cooper: It's been a pleasure. My pleasure.

Q: Thank you very much.

Interview Number 2 with Mr. George C. Cooper
Date: Monday, 18 July 1988
Place: Mr. Cooper's home in Dayton, Ohio
Interviewer: Paul Stillwell

Q: Mr. Cooper, it's a real pleasure to see you again. I've reviewed the transcript recently from our first interview in 1986, and I can see some areas where I think it would be useful to go into greater detail on your experiences.

To start at the beginning, could you tell me more of what it was like growing up as one of ten children? How do you sort out responsibilities and so forth?

Mr. Cooper: Well, that _was_ quite an experience. I think that if any of us amounted to anything, any of the ten of us who lived--one died shortly after she was born--it was because of the kind of parents that we had and the kind of home that those parents provided for us.

One of the things that I think of quite frequently now, and I've been thinking of it more recently than before, has to do with Sunday mornings. Before we would go to Sunday school and church, even before breakfast, my father and mother would call all of us down to the dining room for family prayer. It's the kind of thing that I, at least to my knowledge, don't see in today's world anymore.

Religion played a great part in that family's life. It played a part, despite the fact that my mother and my father went to separate churches. My mother was a member of the Baptist Church, my father was Methodist, and all of the kids went to the Methodist Church. None of us went with Mama.

Q: Why do you think that was?

Mr. Cooper: I don't know. I don't know. It just happened. But it created no confusion and no animosity. Mama was perfectly happy and contented with the whole thing. And it had nothing to do with the religious orientation in the home; it was a joint effort on both parts, on the part of both Mom and Pa. But certainly that had something to do with it.

Another thing, and I think I alluded to this in the initial interview, is the fact that from each of their points of view, the most important thing in life was to get an education. You just had to keep going. High school was not the end of it, despite the fact that neither of them completed high school. Neither of them really ever got out of the lower grades, third, fourth grades.

Q: Why do you think they put such a value on education?

Mr. Cooper: My father read everything he could get his hands on. And I suspect he was as close to a self-educated person as one could find.

Q: What sorts of things did he read?

Mr. Cooper: Pop read everything he could get his hands on. For instance, Papa would read the newspaper from cover to cover, something that I never got around to doing in my life. I envy my wife, because she does it now, even now. But he read history. He was something of a historian. Because of that and because of the things that he exposed himself to, he was able to work with us individually as we tried to do our homework, particularly in areas that he could become reasonably proficient in, based on his reading.

That was not true with Mama. Mama was a housewife, worked her fingers to the bone, not only trying to keep the family together and keep us together as a unit, but helping everybody in the neighborhood. We had a garden in every vacant spot in a five-block area, and she just fed the neighborhood, basically. If somebody came by and Miss Laura thought that that person was hungry, or if that person said he or she was hungry, Mama fed them.

Q: What we now know as welfare was much more a private

thing back then.

Mr. Cooper: Oh, yes, exactly. There was no such thing as a welfare system as we know it today, and people just helped each other. And she was one of the forerunners in providing that kind of help. Fortunately, Pop made a good living, a decent living in his sheet-metal shop. And with the gardens and a cow, we were never hungry. We were well provided for.

Q: Do you know what motivated his reading? Was it just a desire to know more, or did he perhaps have an aspiration to go into some other line of work?

Mr. Cooper: I suspect that if he had had the opportunity, he might have gone into politics. Another big thing in those days, even bigger than today, were lodges. He was a big Mason. In the Masonic Order, he was a worshipful master and demonstrated the kind of leadership ability which showed up not only in that arena, but also in church. He was an elder in the church and took a real leadership position in whatever he was involved in. He was even a volunteer fireman, for instance, which, incidentally, was a little rare in those days, to have a black volunteer fireman. But he was a member of the original fire department in this town of little Washington, North

Cooper #2 - 78

Carolina, because originally it was a volunteer department, as most of them were.

Q: Did he have a position of leadership in the fire department?

Mr. Cooper: I don't recall that. That was long before my time. I just remember hearing them talk about the fact that he was a volunteer fireman.

Q: Well, it's obvious that you have qualities of leadership also, and it could well be that you inherited a number of those from him.

Mr. Cooper: I think that if I or any of my brothers and sisters amounted to anything, it was because of him.

Q: Did you consciously pattern yourself on your father?

Mr. Cooper: Well, as a matter of fact, I was the one child who would go to the shop and work with him, and started my career as a sheet-metal worker. I think I mentioned that in the other interview. It happened that we had run-ins, because I wanted to do things one way and he wanted to do them his way, and, again, as I said in the other interview, when it became evident that we would be better off parting ways, he did everything he could do to help me get started in this little shop that I opened in Wilson, North Carolina. There was never any animosity, always helpfulness, support.

Q: Did you consciously use him as a role model for your own life?

Mr. Cooper: I think so, decidedly so. I used my daddy as a role model and three teachers, one I had in high school and a couple in college.* So that those, I think, were my four role models, Pop first.

Q: In what ways did he demonstrate this leadership in the church setting?

Mr. Cooper: It was one of three of the larger churches in little Washington, black churches, that is, African Methodist Episcopal Zion Church. He helped build it, literally, in terms of not only doing the sheet-metal work in the church, but actually in terms of raising the money—spearheading the activity to raise the money to do it. He was just a pillar in the church.

---

*The high school teacher was Mr. Cox, and the college teachers were William M. Cooper and Herbert King.

Q: Did he and your mother impart to you and the other children the sense of values and ethics that have stayed with you through life?

Mr. Cooper: No question about that, decidedly so.

Q: What sort of specific lessons did they impart?

Mr. Cooper: It was very clear, especially from Mama, that if you had anything and somebody else needed some of it, you had a responsibility to share it. Again, this was more her than him. Pop felt that it was his responsibility to provide for that family, to go out and make the living, which he did to the best of his ability. And, in my judgment, he did a pretty good job of it, because we were one of the very few black families in that little town who owned their own home. That was obviously because of him and because of the kind of people that Mom and Pop were.

One of the other things besides the garden was that we had a cow, and we used to sell milk. Each of us at various stages in our lives had to deliver that milk and deliver vegetables that came from the garden, either downtown to a store or individual customers that my parents had. Frequently, Mama would say, "Stop by So-and-so's house and drop this off, because I know she needs it, and just tell her that Miss Laura sent it." When this kind of thing happens, when you become a part of it and it happens time and time again, it begins to have some meaning for you. I mean, just by osmosis you pick up something. But I think it's important to point out that this was more her influence than his.

Q: What sort of lessons did you get in the work ethic?

Mr. Cooper: I think very fundamentally it came out that the only thing that anybody's going to pay for in life is production. You've got to produce if you're going to make it, which means hard work. And he worked hard, my dad did. He would go home after he closed the shop and have dinner. If he had something else that he needed to do, he'd go back to the shop and finish it or work on it in the evening. Frequently I'd go back with him, even when I was a little tot. Because, as I say, I was the only one who would even pick up a hammer.

Q: Was there a division of chores in the home?

Mr. Cooper: Oh, yes. Of course, they sort of were hand-me-downs, like clothing. For instance, now it's my turn to start milking the cow, and now it's my turn to deliver milk, my turn to go out and pick vegetables, whatever needed to be done around the house. Each one of us had our responsibilities. There was no question about whether or not you were going to do it. You haven't lived, my friend, until you've had a wet dishrag go across the front of your face. (Laughter) If you didn't do what Mama said, you were in trouble. And if you didn't do what Mama said, all she had to do was say, "Wait 'til your Papa comes." And man, you turned tail.

Q: So I'd say discipline is another lesson that was imparted.

Mr. Cooper: You'd better believe it.

Q: Did that grow into self-discipline?

Mr. Cooper: Well, it had to. Yes, it had to. Again, whatever you are, a lot of it goes back to home.

Q: Sure.

Mr. Cooper: And that's one of the things that saddens us, Peg and me, so much today, is to see how the family has just fallen apart. The family structure seems to mean so little in our society today.

Q: That's the so-called "me-first" generation.

Mr. Cooper: Yes.

Q: I grew up with one brother, and I know how that goes. Can you describe what it's like when there are ten siblings? How do you coexist in the same space?

Mr. Cooper: Well, I don't remember how many of us were there at one time, but the ten of them were spaced, obviously, over a period of 15 years, at least, I would think. So that by the time that Clarence comes along, all the rest of them--seven of them--have gone on their merry way. I do remember, however, that we had our ups and downs. On Sunday afternoons, the fad was to walk over to the bridge and walk across the bridge with your girlfriend, if you were fortunate enough to have one. And my younger brother Clarence would always tail along. And at the appropriate time, he would come up and say, "George, Mama said for you to come home. It's time to milk the cow." Well, that's a hell of a thing to say when you were out with your girlfriend! (Laughter) Invariably, he'd pull stunts like this, and we'd have a little squabble and a little spat, and maybe even a little fight. But it didn't mean anything.

Q: Would you describe it as a happy childhood?

Mr. Cooper: Oh, yes. No question about it. Very happy.

Q: How much interaction was there with the church, other than just these sermons and services you went to with your father?

Mr. Cooper: There was certainly more interaction than I see in today's church. We were very active in Sunday school. There was a very active youth group beyond the Sunday school. And it would not be unusual for us to go back to church twice a month for a youth service.

I can remember very vividly one of the ministers we had was blind, literally blind. And I can remember sitting anywhere in that church, depending on what occasion it was, and watching him, and just sitting there saying, "Now, I wonder if he's going to fall off that pulpit." But he never did. The whole time that I was exposed to him, he never slipped or fell. And I wondered how that could possibly be, because this man was totally blind. One of the things that I remember very distinctly was coming to the conclusion, finally, that God must have taken care of him. God had to be with him, because he would get worked up in a sermon, and if you know anything about the old black preachers, they really got emotional about this business, and some still do, incidentally. But to see him romp up and down that pulpit and never miss a step, God had to be on his side.

Q: Did that help give you a sense of ethics, the church experience? How did that relate to home, as far as getting that ingrained?

Mr. Cooper: Well, you tie that in with the fact that every Sunday morning before we went either to Sunday school or church, we'd have family prayer. They obviously went together hand in hand. And you had a sense of religion and a sense of godliness from both sides. It was just ingrained in all of us. It was just a part of our upbringing and a part of our teaching, both at home and abroad.

Q: Did the teaching from your parents also include race relations?

Mr. Cooper: I'm sure it did, but I don't know if we were aware that that's what it was. Obviously, most of the customers that we had, both in terms of produce and in terms of my father's business, were white--I would suggest 90%. And, as I alluded to in the last interview, it was unheard of for a black man to have his own sheet-metal shop. He made tobacco flues, he did all the work for many of the rich families in little Washington, and we were living in a time of strict adherence to discrimination. So that without even knowing what you were doing, you observed your parents operate in that kind of an atmosphere, and do it with a sense of real dignity and real self-worth, which just had to rub off on you. And without realizing what you were confronted with, you'd see people operate in a situation where race relations are handled, and you don't even know they're being handled, if that makes any sense.

Q: It does. So I guess they gave you a sense of pride also.

Mr. Cooper: Oh, golly, yes.

Q: Self-worth.

Mr. Cooper: Self-worth, yes.

Q: Were any of the recipients of the kindnesses from your mother white?

Mr. Cooper: Yes. It didn't make any difference to her. Made no difference to Mama at all. One of our grandmothers was--if she wasn't white, I don't know what she was. She was obviously a black lady, but she was as white as driven snow. And this thread runs through most black families. I suspect in all black families this thread runs through it, and it's not our fault; it was their fault. Even members of your own family who looked like they were white, it didn't make any difference. You finally got to the point where you thought of people as individuals. I think we were able to do that, as a race, better than whites, simply by virtue of the kind of exposure that we had and the kinds of things that we had to put up with. We were, as a race, downtrodden, and there were poor whites who were as downtrodden as we, and I think we had a better appreciation for where they were coming from than they of where we were coming from.

Q: Did the Depression have any impact on your family?

Mr. Cooper: I think it had less on our family than on most families, and I think one of the reasons for it was that when the Depression hit, several of the older ones had gone through college and were out working. Fortunately, none of us had to ever send anything back home to keep the home fires burning. Papa was able to manage to do that, to keep that going. But each of us did, in fact, help each other in terms of going to school beyond high school. And, as I say, each of us got at least a college degree. So that when the Depression hit, there were enough of us out that we were able to continue sending the appropriate one to college and that kind of thing. I'm sure it had some effect, but I don't recall any disastrous effects that the Depression had on the family.

Q: When did you first come to an awareness of the racial injustices that existed?

Mr. Cooper: I suppose somewhere along the time when that little boy I mentioned in the last interview called me a nigger the wrong day when I was going downtown. We obviously recognized it by the time we went to the first grade. There was no such thing as going to kindergarten, no day-care centers then. You certainly recognized it when you walked in the first time to go to school, and it's all black, and you know that there are other kinds of people in this town. Where are they? You recognized that you were black, and knew that there was a segregated society from infancy, almost.

Q: But that's where it first becomes so apparent. Did white and black children play together, for example? Prejudice is something that has to be taught. It's not innate.

Mr. Cooper: No, it is, in fact, taught.

Our parents were determined to instill the work ethic in us, so we children used to go out, for instance, and work on farms in the tobacco fields. I can remember, as a youngster, working in tobacco fields, handing tobacco. (When you hand it, you pick up three leaves and hand it to the person who ties it.) And these would be adults. They would frequently bring their kids to work with them, because they didn't have any place to leave them. They'd bring the kids to the farm, and they'd sit on the ground until Mama got through working. You'd see these black kids playing with the farmers' kids, for instance, and there was that kind of interaction. And you'd note that kind of thing go on until you got up to a certain age, and then there would be a separation, and it would be very clear. I mean, after a certain period, you don't have anything to do with these people.

Q: That was that era's version of the day-care center.

Mr. Cooper: I suppose so, yes. But beyond that, never the twain shall meet.

Q: Was there any overt hostility that you remember as a youngster, other than that one case you cited?

Mr. Cooper: Oh, yes. One of the things I did at the time

I started high school, I worked as a bellhop in a hotel to make some extra money. I did it after high school in an effort to get enough money to help go to college. Obviously, the people who were traveling and staying in hotels in little Washington, North Carolina, were, for the most part, sales people--drummers, we called them. And the hostility that you would encounter there would just make your hair stand on edge. Hostility not because you did anything to anybody, but hostility simply because of prejudice and because of the fact that you were black.

Q: Do you remember any specific cases?

Mr. Cooper: I remember one situation, for instance, where I was helping a man register, showing him to his room, and started in the elevator. I had put his bags in the elevator, and he tried to get on the elevator. This is one of the elevators where the operator opens and closes the door; it didn't do it automatically. And this guy inadvertently got caught in the door the wrong way. I thought the man was going to hit me, really. He called me everything he could think of, everything derogatory that came to his mind. From my perspective it was obviously an accident. But if anything went wrong in the lobby, it was considered your fault as the bellhop. It was never the manager's fault, who was behind the desk. That kind of thing was just a part of living, just a part of being there.

Q: Some people, whether they're dealing with a black or white bellhop, feel some air of superiority, and that was probably part of the relationship, too, that, "I've hired this service, and so you're working for me."

Mr. Cooper: Yes. Except that at that particular point in time, in my lifetime, in my experience, however, all the bellhops were black. There were no white bellhops.

Q: The drummers and other people would come in expecting you to be subservient, I presume. How do you square that with your notion of self-pride?

Mr. Cooper: Pride is certainly a good thing to have and something that every person should have, but I think that in any person's lifetime, there are innumerable occasions when one has to swallow that pride to do what one thinks he needs to do and has to do if he's going to really accomplish anything in life. I sincerely believe that.

Q: What do you remember about your school years? Were there any subjects that you were especially good at?

Mr. Cooper: I liked mathematics, didn't like physics, didn't like chemistry particularly. But math was my forte, and I just thoroughly and completely enjoyed that. I enjoyed languages and English, participated in college and in high school in dramatics, and I got a big kick out of that. I suppose there was a lot of ham in me, the kind of ham that I see, for instance, today in our granddaughter. I think she came by it naturally. I suppose because of that, I did, in fact, enjoy English and literature and that kind of thing. But math was my best subject.

Q: You said before that in retrospect, it wasn't all that good an education. How much preparation would you say the teachers had?

Mr. Cooper: The teachers were obviously poorly prepared, simply by virtue of the fact that they hadn't been prepared in a good college. See, when I came along, and when I started in school, I don't know if many of the teachers really had a college education. I suspect that the most that they had done was what they called in those days a normal school, which is the equivalent now, I suppose, to about two years of college in an associate degree program in today's educational world. Now a lot of those people, simply by virtue of their desire to be good in whatever area they were teaching, had gone beyond to study more and try to put that over to their students. But I suspect I was in high school before I had some teacher who had really completed college, a four-year college course.

Q: Did any of them create in you a love of learning?

Mr. Cooper: Yes, there was--especially one in high school--a Mr. Cox. I talked to my sisters about him the last time I was in Washington, to see if he was still alive. He was the personification of dignity, one of the best reared men I have ever known. He had one arm. He thought he saw some potential, I suppose, and he sort of took me under his wing. He had me in speaking contests and all this sort of thing, and he would tutor me. He was a real influence in my life. He was, as I say, one of the four people that I perceived of as role models.

Q: What subject did he teach?

Mr. Cooper: He taught history, which was one of my worst subjects. But he, again, apparently saw some potential there and worked with me quite hard and quite diligently.

Q: Did the curriculum include an emphasis on black history?

Mr. Cooper: No. I don't recall a single class in black history until college, actually, and that's strange. I never thought of it before. But as I think back on it, I don't recall any emphasis on black history until I got to college.

Q: Did your parents make sure you got your homework?

Mr. Cooper: Oh, Lord, yes. There's no question about that. Doing homework was a ritual in this household, just part of every day, because you weren't going back to school tomorrow and embarrass Mama and Papa by not having done your homework. You know, if you screwed up at school and you got a whipping at school, you'd get another one when you got home. The one at school was the first one. (Laughter) You were sure to get a second one when you got home if word got there before you did. So that they were strict disciplinarians, my parents were.

Q: And maybe you'd get three if Mom got to you before Dad did.

Mr. Cooper: Exactly. That's right. Yes, because she was there when you got home; he wasn't there from work yet.

Q: Did you have heroes as a youngster?

Mr. Cooper: Well, I suspect my first hero was Mr. Cox, when I was in high school, the fellow I just mentioned to you.

Q: I'm thinking also of people in the larger world that you read about or heard about on the radio.

Mr. Cooper: As I said earlier, my father read an awful lot. As a matter of fact, we had one room in our house which was called the library, and there were a fair number of books in that room, with a piano, because all of my brothers and sisters played the piano. So that we did, in fact, have heroes that we read about. There was some black history among the books there, you know, even in those days. So that we knew about people, Marcus Garvey, for instance.* I can remember my father and mother talking about Marcus Garvey and people like that who were, in fact, black heroes. That's another funny thing. You never hear about people like that anymore today, except in occasions like over the past weekend when we had the black cultural festival here in Dayton, and you bring out names of this kind which were heroes when I was coming along.

---
*Marcus Garvey (1887-1940) was a Jamaican-born black nationalist leader who came to the United States in 1916. He founded the Universal Negro Improvement Association and several businesses.

Q: What about Booker T. Washington?* Was he one of those that you read about?

Mr. Cooper: Yes. Booker T. Washington, when I was coming up, had just started Tuskegee, you see, and Mary McLeod Bethune, of course, was one of the educators that you read an awful lot about, because she had started Bethune-Cookman College along at about that time in history. So that you had these kinds of people to whom you obviously looked up. And your parents would say, "Well now, you know, these people can do it, you can do it. You can, in fact, be whatever you want to be if you get yourself prepared to do it."

Q: Did you read for pleasure?

Mr. Cooper: Yes.

Q: What sorts of things, other than history?

Mr. Cooper: Well, I liked fiction and I still do, with a

---

*Booker Taliaferro Washington (1856-1915) was educated at Hampton Institute in the early 1870s. In 1881 he founded, at Tuskegee, Alabama, the Tuskegee Institute for the practical training of blacks in trades and professions. It became one of the best-known of all black colleges. He was elected to the American Hall of Fame in 1945.

sort of a fondness for mysteries. Most of my reading, honestly, was light reading. I'm not an intellectual.

Q: What else did you do for recreation?

Mr. Cooper: Played baseball out in a lot, you know, a sandlot, touch football, marbles. You never shot marbles; you're too young, I suspect.

Q: Not very much. I did a little bit.

Mr. Cooper: But playing marbles was a big thing when I was growing up. It was a hobby. It wasn't an expensive thing. As a matter of fact, both boys and girls played a lot of jacks when I was coming up, because it didn't cost too much to engage in the sport. I got fairly proficient at shooting marbles.

Q: Were you involved in any sports in school?

Mr. Cooper: No. No, the nearest thing I came to sports in school was a cheerleader.

Q: Well, it's interesting. That's one of the few common threads I've seen in the members of the Golden Thirteen, that quite a number were very good athletes.

Mr. Cooper: You're right. But I was not one of them.

Q: What sorts of extracurricular activities did you get into in school?

Mr. Cooper: Well, I was the president of the debating society, for instance. I enjoyed that thoroughly. As a matter of fact, there's a friend of mine in Dayton now. She was at Morgan State when I was at Hampton Institute, and we used to debate--the two schools together.* We get together frequently, almost every time we see each other, and reminisce about those good old days. I was a member of the Hampton Players. I sang as a member of the Hampton Institute choir and as a member of the Hampton quartet. So those were the kinds of extracurricular activities that I participated in.

Q: What were some of the issues that you debated? Do you recall them?

Mr. Cooper: That's been 50 years ago. That's a long time.

Q: I'm always amazed at the things that stick in people's memories.

---
*Morgan College, Baltimore, Maryland.

Mr. Cooper: Fifty years ago.

Q: How much did you keep up with world events in those years?

Mr. Cooper: We had debates around world events, as a matter of fact, and I suspect that was a part of the educational process. If you're going to have a debating team on a college campus, you obviously took current events as one of the many subject matters with which you would deal in the business of debating. But, again, it's been so long ago, I don't remember any details.

Q: I think the League of Nations was a debate topic, among other things, back then.*

Mr. Cooper: There you go. Yes. You've reminded me.

Q: Did you debate racial topics, do you think?

Mr. Cooper: I don't recall that we did the racial things. I think they were more current event kinds of things.

Q: Where in the hierarchy of bigotry and so forth would

---

*The League of Nations, comparable to the current United Nations, was established in the wake of World War I. It lasted until the mid-1930s, when it came apart under the international tensions that later resulted in World War II.

the state of North Carolina fit? Was that deep South? How would you rank it?

Mr. Cooper: I think I would rank North Carolina as deep South. Yes, deep South. Washington, North Carolina, was a rough old town to grow up in.

Q: In what ways?

Mr. Cooper: Well, today, for instance, you at least hope that you have a police force composed of people with some sort of training to be police officers. You picked up somebody and put a badge on him, when I was coming up in little Washington, North Carolina. And you had difficulty with almost everybody you ran into who was white, simply because you were black.

Q: What kinds of difficulties?

Mr. Cooper: You couldn't, for instance, go in a store and try anything on. You could go in a store and buy a pair of shoes, size six or whatever. You go in a store and you try a six-and-a-half hat, and that's your hat. Once you put it on your head, that's your hat. Obviously, there's no such thing as going into a white drugstore and sitting down at the fountain and having a Coke. You could buy an ice cream cone and take it out, or you could buy a drink and take it out, which is, I suppose, the reason that we had a black drugstore in this little town. The people who ran the place made a good living at it.

Q: Were there cases of violence?

Mr. Cooper: Oh, sure. We never got involved in any real violent situations in terms of our own family, but I can recall case after case of violence in terms of white and black. I can even remember two lynchings as a youngster, not too far from home. Beatings, particularly in my early childhood. Again, it never happened to us, I suspect because of the kind of relationship that our family had and the kind of home life that we had, because our parents protected us. They probably overprotected us, if that's possible. But we were never out on the streets, we never hung around with street gangs or anything like that. We stuck pretty much to home, studies, church. So we were, in fact, protected.

Q: Did you feel intimidated by these things you heard about, the lynchings and so forth?

Mr. Cooper: There's no question. You had to feel

intimidated by it, because you recognized two or three things. First of all, that it was done simply on the basis of prejudice, for the most part; secondly, there wasn't a hell of a lot you could do about it; and thirdly, because I think at that point in time, there was no groundswell from the majority community to try to do anything about it. You know, a Rainbow Coalition would have been just unmentionable.* You wouldn't even mention such a thing as a Rainbow Coalition in those days.

Q: Well, the one thing that you could do was avoid the kinds of situations that precipitated them, so that you don't become a victim yourself.

Mr. Cooper: You did that religiously. You did that as a matter of course. There's no question about that.

Q: I would suspect that some of these things weren't even verbalized; it was just part of what you absorbed with growing up.

Mr. Cooper: You just came by it naturally, just doing what's natural--as unnatural as it was. You didn't even think about it. And these kids today don't know what the

---

*The term "Rainbow Coalition" was used to describe the support by people of various colors for Jesse Jackson's 1988 presidential candidacy.

hell prejudice is, and there's still institutional racism abounding in our society, but these kids don't even know how to spell it, compared to what we went through as kids and what our parents went through.

Q: What led to your choice of Hampton as a place to go to college?

Mr. Cooper: Four of my brothers and sisters ahead of me had gone to Hampton, and I just thought that was the thing to do. In the second place, they had a trade school. Hampton and Tuskegee were the only two trade schools I knew anything about, and I wanted to follow in my dad's footsteps as a sheet-metal worker. They had a sheet-metal program at Hampton, as they did at Tuskegee, but Hampton was closer to home, and so I elected to go to Hampton.

Q: How would you characterize the quality of the faculty there?

Mr. Cooper: I think that Hampton Institute, in those days, was probably one of the top institutions in the country in terms of black colleges, Hampton and Tuskegee. Howard and Morgan, close seconds, in my judgment.*

Q: That's interesting, that you put it ahead of Howard.

---

*Howard University, Washington, D. C.

Mr. Cooper: You know, I think there's a reason for it. When I was in college at Hampton, the faculty was predominantly white. There were more white faculty than black faculty, and it is my judgment that because of that, the quality of Hampton's faculty was probably a little bit better than an all-black faculty in a black institution, because their exposure had been broader. I think it was natural to expect that that would be the case. I don't think that says anything against the black faculty, because they were exposed to what they were exposed to. The white faculty had been exposed to so much broader an educational process. It was so much broader and so much better, if you will, so that I think that at Hampton we had a better faculty than some of the other black colleges. Many of those people were really dedicated people.

Q: Graham Martin said that he did his undergraduate work at Ohio State, then he went to Howard for a master's, and he thought it would be a breeze. And he was surprised at how difficult it was, that it was much more challenging than he expected. And so he had gotten the white view of Howard, and it was kind of a jolt to him to face the reality.

Mr. Cooper: Well, I can remember--and my wife and I talk

about this frequently, because she remembers from her undergraduate days at Wilberforce--there were certain scholars on black university campuses who really stood out--Alain Locke, for instance.* A friend of ours who just died recently, J. Saunders Redding, is another example, as is my son-in-law's father, Allison Davis.** You had these kinds of people who stood out on black campuses and who were really exceptional, some of whom had even studied in Europe, despite all the segregation and all the other stuff. They had risen above whatever it was and had gone on. So that you had these scattered throughout black universities, colleges and universities across the country. And to have that kind of exposure would mean a great deal to a person.

Q: How did you benefit from this capable faculty at Hampton?

Mr. Cooper: Part of the ethic at Hampton was drop down your bucket where you are, and it came from Booker T. Washington. I suppose General Armstrong, when he founded

---
*Alain L. Locke (1886-1954) was professor of philosophy at Howard University and author of a number of books, including The New Negro (1925).
**J. Saunders Redding (1906-1988) was the author of numerous books and held teaching positions at several universities; he was a full professor at Cornell University when he retired. Allison Davis (1902-1986) was the author of several works of social anthropology and psychology; he served as John Dewey distinguished service professor at the University of Chicago.

Hampton Institute, had that same kind of thing in his mind, and he had, therefore, built an atmosphere on that campus that supported what I had alluded to earlier in terms of where I came from out of the family: that if you really worked at it, you could do it, but you had to work at it. There was no free ride in society. If you put forth the effort and got something in your head, you could accomplish something and come reasonably close to fulfilling your potential as a human being and an individual. And you could do that in spite of the fact that there was segregation and discrimination and racial conflict.

Q: Did the white teachers treat the black students with respect?

Mr. Cooper: Oh, yes, at Hampton, particularly, and I suspect at other institutions, too, because I don't think these were people who took a job at Hampton because they couldn't get one somewhere else. These were dedicated people, for the most part. And I can remember many of them for whom you have the utmost respect. And they obviously were not working there for salary; they were working there out of commitment.

Q: Well, the very fact that they were there then speaks

well.

Mr. Cooper: Yes.

Q: What did you study besides your specialty in sheet-metal work?

Mr. Cooper: We had courses in general education, English, history, chemistry, if that's what you mean.

Q: Yes.

Mr. Cooper: As a matter of fact, I got a degree in what we called trade education, which qualified me to teach, and so I had to take a lot of general education courses in order to qualify for the degree. If you just got a diploma as having graduated from a trade school, you didn't have to do as much general education. But going toward a degree, you had to meet those degree requirements.

Q: In our first interview, you talked about some of the things you did to get money to pay for your education. Did you also get some financial help from your parents?

Mr. Cooper: I got a little financial help from my parents, but most of the financial help that I got outside came from my older brothers and sisters. And, again, this was instilled in us as we were coming up: "When you get out, you help the next one."

Q: Did they find success in later life, your brothers and sisters?

Mr. Cooper: I think so. My oldest brother, Edward, for instance, was head of the Urban League in Boston. He was the first black manager of a supermarket in Boston. All four of my sisters--Helen, Louise, Ruth, and Lillie--were schoolteachers. I had another brother, Robert, who ran a school for delinquent boys in upstate New York; he was a social worker and died as a result of directing an anti-poverty program called Har-You-Act in Harlem. I really think that's what killed him. I had another brother, Cornelius, in New York, who owned and operated his own liquor store as a business. Clarence, a brother younger than I, was a reasonably well-known folksinger before he died 12 years ago.

Q: Quite a range of occupations there.

You talked about the singing trips that you went on and drove, as well. Did that have a broadening experience for you?

Mr. Cooper: Oh, yes, because it exposed you to so many different kinds of situations, both in terms of situations and in terms of people. For instance, we would go on one singing trip as a sort of fund-raising effort, and that would obviously attract a certain kind of person to the performance. We'd go to the Chamberlin Hotel, right there on the point at Fort Monroe, and we'd sing just for the hotel crowd, which would attract a different kind of clientele, obviously. So that you had different situations and different people with whom you came into contact, and you learned from all of these experiences. From each different kind of exposure, you learned something else.

Q: What kinds of audiences did these include that you sang for?

Mr. Cooper: Well, for instance, the Chamberlin was a fairly sophisticated and fairly high-class hotel. It was within five or six miles of the campus. It was a pretty high-class audience. They were obviously all white, and the hotel would provide this as entertainment for their guests after dinner. And we'd go out and sing for a group like that.

Then we would go to a place like Richmond or a place like Charlotte, and sing for a smaller, private gathering of people that the fund-raisers would arrange in an effort to try to raise money for the school. That's a different kind of clientele altogether. And, again, because they were different clienteles, you'd learn different things from them, and you'd respond to them differently.

Q: What were some of the things you learned?

Mr. Cooper: For instance, from one of the things where you would go to and sing as a fund-raising effort, you would recognize that there were people in the world who were interested in perpetuating education and particularly, in this case, education for blacks, and were, therefore, willing to put some money behind that. On occasions of that nature, sometimes it was possible to have social interaction with them. Frequently it was possible to do that.

You began to recognize in situations like that, that there are good people in the world. In spite of prejudice, in spite of discrimination, there are people who are really concerned and people who care, and people who are willing to put their money where their mouth is and try to make a difference. In my judgment, that had a tendency in those times to make you go into a situation where you would walk into a hotel and simply sing for money, you know, because they'd pay you to come in. See, you're just an entertainer. It didn't make any difference if a drunk talked the whole time you were singing or whatever. You learned to cope with that, because you needed that extra $10.00 to help pay next month's bills at school.

You, a few minutes ago, said, "How much support did you get from your parents?" We got a lot of support. I can remember writing home and saying to Papa I needed some money to buy a pair of shoes. And you could get a pair of Thom McAn shoes then for $3.15. He'd send you three dollars and say, "You ought to be able to get the 15 cents yourself," and he was serious. So that the ten dollars that you made singing at the Chamberlin Hotel meant a lot.

Q: What sort of repertoire did the group have? What songs did you sing?

Mr. Cooper: For the most part, we sang spirituals. Ninety-five percent of our repertoire was spirituals. We had a faculty person at Hampton who was in charge of the group and taught us. He was quite a musician.

You'd have similar kinds of experiences when you traveled as a member of the Hampton Institute Choir. Those were the good old days.

Q: Did you keep up with the events in Europe and so forth as that continent moved closer to war?

Mr. Cooper: Yes. You were aware of what was going on. Sure.

Q: Did you have the feeling then that the United States would become involved?

Mr. Cooper: Oh, I had the feeling that I didn't see how they could not become involved. They had to become involved. Not only did you have that kind of feeling, but you recognized that eventually you would have to become involved in some form or another. You know, in those days, you didn't hear about draft dodgers. You just went in. It was just part of the game. So that you knew you'd eventually have to become personally involved at the appropriate time.

Q: When you left with your degree, did you have long-range goals in mind?

Mr. Cooper: Actually, when I left with my degree, I wasn't particularly interested in teaching, even though I was qualified and certified to teach. I wanted to go in business for myself, and as I indicated in the other interview, I wanted to make metal caskets. I just couldn't swing it. Then I ended up teaching, you know, because I had to make a living.

Cooper #2 - 113

Q: But I'm wondering if you saw metal caskets as a lifetime goal, or was there something beyond that, that you were thinking about?

Mr. Cooper: I wanted to be an entrepreneur, and that was a way to get there. My father had been in business before me, had done reasonably well in terms of providing for his family and making a living for his family and, again, was one of my role models. And I felt that business was the route to take, and in business for myself.

Q: You've also said that one of the problems you would have had with the Navy is that people were there telling you where to go and what to do. You envisioned, obviously, being your own boss in this business world.

Mr. Cooper: Oh, yes. Oh, yes. But, as things turned out, it didn't happen that way. I was in business for a very short period of time, and this was right before World War II. And then after service, I stayed in education and public service except for my business experience with Crawford.*

Q: You said that the one thing that facilitated this sheet-metal work was your manual dexterity. Were there

---

*In the first interview, Mr. Cooper describes working in a cleaning business with Mr. Cal Crawford of Dayton, Ohio.

other examples from the time you were growing up, of things you made?

Mr. Cooper: The only things I can think of that I made, if I understand your question, were things that were made right there in the shop with my dad. I subsequently developed some facility in crafts. For instance, one of my hobbies now is jewelry-making, because I still like to use my hands. I get a great deal of pleasure out of that; I can forget everything when I'm working with my hands. I was working with some jewelry last night, as recently as last night. You get frustrated and you go back and play with some rocks; it makes you feel like a different person. You forget your troubles sometimes.

Q: Did you make a crystal radio, model airplanes, things of that sort?

Mr. Cooper: I tried crystal radios. That was about the extent of it. I never went into model airplanes.

Q: What about erector sets or building blocks?

Mr. Cooper: Oh, yes, we had that kind of thing, but I thought you meant making something from scratch. Building blocks and that kind of thing, yes.

Q: And I'm sure part of the pleasure of these trips to your dad's shop at night was just being with him.

Mr. Cooper: Oh, yes. We had a good relationship. I sort of felt that he and I had a better relationship than any of my brothers, and I suspect that was natural because I was the one of the sons that would work with him. The rest of them had no desire, no interest in this kind of thing at all. That probably accounted for much of it, because I enjoyed it. Not just him, but doing the work, too.

Q: You talked before about going to Hampton to teach in the Navy school. Did you see this as an alternative to military service?

Mr. Cooper: Yes, as a matter of fact, I did. The draft board was breathing down my neck.

Q: Had the war started yet?

Mr. Cooper: Yes, and I had an opportunity to interview for this job. As a matter of fact, at that point in time, I was working here in what was called National Youth Administration, teaching aircraft sheet-metal work at a college over near Xenia, Wilberforce University. I felt when this opportunity came to teach metalsmiths at a naval installation that I'd have a better opportunity of working as a civilian than I would working over here in NYA as a civilian. And that's really the reason I took the job.

Q: What was your reason for preferring to be a civilian--because of the discrimination you knew in the military?

Mr. Cooper: I think that had something to do with it. I think that a larger part of it was the fact that I had a feeling, rightly or wrongly, that in the military you were not your own boss. I mean, you did what you were ordered to do. And to that extent, you were subject to other people's whims, and I always liked the idea of being my own boss to the extent possible. Obviously, if you're working, you've got a boss, even in civilian life. But, you know, you're not ordered today to leave tomorrow and go to Timbuktu in a civilian situation.

Q: You talked before about dealing creatively with the racial situation as a personnel officer. Were there other examples, before you got into the Navy, in which you tried to do that? You cited the fact of bringing individuals in, as a personnel officer, and letting them see you and get to know you as an individual. Had you done that sort of thing earlier?

Mr. Cooper: I'd done it earlier and later, and still do it. If, for instance, there's a need to try to influence somebody and influence them creatively, along the lines we're discussing, I think the best way you can do that is to have a personal interaction with that person. That person then comes to know you and work with you as a person around an object, around an idea, around a desire. In terms of one on one, if you get to know me as George Cooper and I get to know you as Paul Stillwell, then prejudice has to break down, because we have found a commonality among us that has brought us together as human beings. I think that's the best way to do it.

I can remember back again in church, as a child--and I don't think this was in the first interview--we used to sing this song "You bring the one next to you, and I'll bring the one next to me, and in no time at all, we'll win them all. We'll win them one by one." And that thing has stuck with me all my life. If I've had any influence in terms of trying to change people's attitudes and minds, it's been on a one-on-one basis--to the extent possible-- because I think that's the best way to do it.

Q: Do you remember any specific cases that you could cite?

Mr. Cooper: I can remember many. For instance, there's a man who is a very good friend of mine in Dayton. Ken was a police officer. And when I first went to work for the city of Dayton, I went to work as a housing inspector. And Ken came on after I got on as a housing inspector. And Ken knew he was better than anybody else. I would find and arrange, deviously, for us to go on inspections together. While we were out on inspection, I might say, "Let's stop by the house and have a hot dog, Ken." And Ken learned to recognize that I lived pretty much like he did. He got to learn that he could appreciate me as a human being and not as a black man, and we developed a real kinship.

I remember, for instance, one of the secretaries in our office, when I was in housing inspection, came and said, "George, I'd like to talk to you."

I said, "Sit down, Jan. Let's talk."

She said, "I took this job because I was really unhappy on the last job I took." She'd been there just two weeks. She said, "When I came in here and saw you sitting behind that desk, I was ready to go back and try to ask for my old job back, because I'd never worked with a black person in my life and felt that I simply couldn't do it."

I said, "Why are you telling me this now? Why are you unburdening your soul to me? You didn't quit, obviously, and you're still here."

She said, "I just wanted to tell you and share with

you, as a result of interaction for just a period of two weeks, I've come to know and recognize you as a human being, and it has taught me that I've been wrong all my life." See? Now, in this case, I made no specific effort to influence this kid. You know, I was just myself.

Q: Living your life.

Mr. Cooper: Living my life and trying to do a job. But you have influenced a human being, another human being, to the point that this young woman came down and sat and talked to you heart to heart, face to face like this. And it says maybe something is worth it. You do things like that. In this case, I never even thought about what I was doing. She said, "You're the only one in the whole office who's been a real gentleman to me since I've been here." She said, "I have a lot of respect for you." Those of us in the office would come in, and we would hand her our work, and she would see the quality of my work and the quality of everybody else's work, and she said that had something to do with it, too.

Q: Were there cases of people who were initially hostile that you won over?

Mr. Cooper: There was another fellow, Russ--again, he was

in the same unit with us in housing inspection. Russ was a bigot of the last order and made no bones about it. He had a particularly difficult case that he was working on, and he would never have come to me to ask for any sort of assistance. He had asked Ken, the guy that I had just alluded to a minute ago, and Ken said, "I really don't know what to do with this thing. Let's go ask George. This is right down his alley. I know he can help us out with this thing."

He said, "Hell, I ain't going to that nigger." (I can hear him now.)

Ken said, "Look, man. You want to straighten this thing out. Now, if you don't want to go to the boss with it, to the chief inspector, you better come on and let's get it straightened out with George, because I think he can help us." And he reluctantly came.

A few weeks later, he brought another case, and then he started saying, "Would you work on this case with me?" He wasn't in love with me, but he respected me.

In 1966, when we had the riots in Dayton, the so-called riots, the Area Progress Council started a thing called the White-Black Committee.* There were a dozen from the real power structure in Dayton and a dozen blacks whom they perceived as leaders in the community. The president of the University of Dayton was the chairperson

---
*The Area Progress Council was comprised of the leaders of the local business community.

of that committee. The second meeting of the committee, he had to be out of town, and asked me if I'd chair it. (I subsequently served on the university's board of directors.) I said that I was going to exercise the prerogative of chair and change the order of business.

The first thing I was going to do was get a name that was appropriate for this committee, because I didn't think Black-White Committee was what it was all about. In introducing that subject, I made comments to the effect that I was aware that institutional racism was alive and well in our community. That was, in fact, the reason for the riots. I was also aware of the fact that, in my judgment, we were not doing this because of any change of heart on the part of the white population or on the part of the power structure; we were doing it because the power structure wanted to protect its interest. And it had an interest to protect: "If you tear up this town, you're tearing up our stuff."

Q: They were scared.

Mr. Cooper: Damn right. And that I thought we ought to have a name that was more appropriate than the Black-White Committee, because if we were just meeting as blacks and whites, just to be meeting together didn't mean anything.

We had to have a program, had to have an agenda. We changed our name at that meeting to the Community Affairs Committee. We have met since then the second Wednesday of every month at 7:30 for breakfast, and have done a lot of things in this community without any fanfare at all. I don't even know why I told you that story. I don't know what brought it to my mind.

Q: Well, I'm glad I heard it. We talked about when you were teaching at Navy metalsmiths at Hampton. What sort of things specifically were you working on?

Mr. Cooper: Partly it was aircraft mechanics. Another part of it was for the shipbuilding industry.

Q: Was there a Navy-developed curriculum that you worked with?

Mr. Cooper: Oh, yes.

Q: What sorts of training aids or shop facilities did you have?

Mr. Cooper: We had good shop facilities, because we used the shop in the trade school at Hampton Institute. It was right there in their shop. We trained our people in their shops, except for boatswains and diesel mechanics. Hampton did not have a diesel shop. The Navy actually set up a diesel shop there. But for the most part, we used the shops that were already in existence in the trade school at Hampton, so that we had a fully equipped sheet-metal shop, and it was adequate for training metalsmiths for the Navy.

Q: How capable were the students you got?

Mr. Cooper: I think they were reasonably capable. They were enlistees and draftees--people who, as a result of interviews had been directed to this assignment. I think because of the fact that the fellows had been selected to go to Class A school, they had some incentive to try a little harder, even if it was difficult for them and something that they didn't particularly like. So that I think they did a reasonably good job in terms of doing the best they could do with it.

Q: The Navy has tests in addition to the interviews, so presumably these men had some aptitude.

Mr. Cooper: They had some aptitude, obviously, yes. That's how they got there, because of the aptitude tests and the interviews that they'd had with the personnel people.

Q: Did you find that a satisfying kind of work?

Mr. Cooper: Yes, it was satisfying, because you were taking young men and having them develop the potential that you saw in them. I've always enjoyed working with people. I think if I have any skills, that's probably one of them, the ability to work with people. I get a great deal of satisfaction out of seeing people grow and develop.

Q: It's interesting that you took the education courses at Hampton not because you planned to use them, but they undoubtedly came in handy here.

Mr. Cooper: Decidedly, yes.

Q: You talked briefly about Commander Downes before. I would welcome anything else you remember about him, specific incidents and what have you.

Mr. Cooper: I can remember that the only time I ever got drunk in my life, I got drunk in the commander's house, in the skipper's house. He would throw the wildest parties you've ever seen. And there were five houses in this little cul-de-sac, and he lived in one and I lived in the third one down. I was living in that house when I was working as a civilian. Then after I got commissioned and went back there to work, I just stayed in my same house. I can remember getting really drunk one night at the skipper's house and walking home and saying to my wife, "Peg, I want to see my baby."

And she said, "If you wake that baby up, I'll kill you." (Laughter) That was one of the big fights that we had, one of the many fights that we had. And I've always attributed that to the skipper, to Commander Downes, for making me drunk at his house, at his party, because he threw some wild parties.

But, again, the thing I remember him most for was the ability he had to remember a person by name and his ability to lead men. He was a real leader of men, in my judgment.

Q: How did he manifest that leadership?

Mr. Cooper: I think he manifested that leadership by demonstrating a sincere interest in you as a person. I saw him work with trainees, ship's company, officers, using the same, the identical techniques and making it work. I think I learned a great deal from him, too.

Q: Was he a fair-minded person?

Mr. Cooper: Yes. He was tough, and he insisted that you

produce, but he was honest and he was fair with you. And I suspect that of all the people that I worked with in the Navy, I probably had as much respect for him as anybody, with the exception of Jack Dille.

Q: It sounds as if Commander Downes was very well suited for being there at that point in time.

Mr. Cooper: I think that they could not have found a better person to have sent to that Class A training school. I really do. I'd even go so far as to say that when he was transferred, the school started going downhill, in my judgment. He was the right man at the right place at the right time.

Q: Why would it go down? What qualities did he have that his successor didn't?

Mr. Cooper: The new man didn't have the quality of leadership. The quality of leadership simply was no longer there. I don't even think the basic intelligence was there. That's harsh, but you asked me, and it's an honest answer.

Q: Did he get promoted to captain while you were at Hampton?

Mr. Cooper: No.

Q: The one story that you told me before that I had a little trouble understanding was this anti-black captain that you met, and then he got transferred to Alaska. It seems to me that that would only work if a visitor was junior to Downes. I mean, how could he get somebody senior to him shipped out?

Mr. Cooper: Let me tell you what I think happened.

Q: All right.

Mr. Cooper: My impression was--and I think this is fairly accurate--that they used this Class A segregated training school at Hampton Institute in Tidewater, Virginia, not just to train black sailors, but to train, if you will, naval personnel in the handling of black enlistees, black naval personnel. So I think they sent people there on temporary assignments to get that kind of exposure. Because, again, I think that the top brass in Washington perceived Downes as being one of the best men in this area that they had in the whole Navy, therefore, capable of helping other people who would have responsibility for doing something with black sailors. There was something to

Cooper #2 - 128

be learned at Hampton, at this Class A training school which Downes ran. I am sure we had a goodly number of people who came in, who were senior to him in terms of rank. This was a part of a training process--several officers each month to be trained in the handling of Negro troops. Scores of officers were involved here.

Q: Well, then, you're not going to achieve any training if you ship the guy right off to Alaska, are you?

Mr. Cooper: No. Well, I don't think that we had many people who would come in and say to the commanding officer something like, "I hope I never see another black guy in my life. I saw this guy you had last night who came to meet me, and he's an officer. I'd just as soon not see another nigger the rest of my life." The whole campus is black. You may as well let this gentleman go right now. I think that was the response that he would naturally take and made it stick.

Q: From the way that you responded to this captain, then, you must have known you would have had Downes's backing.

Mr. Cooper: No question. I knew that I had Downes's backing. Oh, Lord, yes. I'd have bet my bottom dollar on that, simply by virtue of the man that I knew he was.

Q: He must have had a fair amount of pull to be able to get you an appointment as a chief petty officer as easily as he did.

Mr. Cooper: That's another consideration. My impression was that he had no problem with that.

Q: When you were made a chief, did you go into a specific rating, or were you a training specialist?

Mr. Cooper: Training specialist.*

Q: I'd be interested how you related to the other chiefs. Did they resent that you had become a chief instantly?

Mr. Cooper: There may have been some of that present, but I don't recall any overt thing. We had two or three, as I recall, old black chiefs, and those guys worked for their rates. It wasn't handed to them on a silver platter. Those guys had gone through hell to get the ratings that they had. And I suspect that there was some normal and natural kinds of resentment, but it was never overtly demonstrated, to my knowledge. I mean, I was never aware

---
*This was one of several specialist ratings created by the Navy during World War II to facilitate the conferring of advanced rates on individuals who were qualified on the basis of their civilian expertise and background.

of it. Again, I sort of had the facility, for some reason or other, to get along with all kinds of people in all kinds of situations. I can remember the chief, for instance, who was in charge of the galley. He became one of my best friends, just a decent human being. Even today, both my wife and me, we have friends in every level of society. I mean, we don't pick our friends based on money or class; we pick our friends based on people, on who you are and what you are as a human being. I really think that that's one of the things that's brought us through and it's helped us through.

When I was a civilian on the faculty at Hampton, we had a bunch of our friends in for a party. A fellow knocked on the door. He ran a fish market in the little town of Hampton. He said, "George, you got a minute?"

I said, "Sure. Come on in."

He opened the door, and he looked in, he said, "Oh, I'm sorry. I didn't realize you had guests."

I said, "Doesn't make any difference. You want to talk privately?"

He said, "Yes."

I said, "Come on upstairs." We went through the living room and upstairs. I don't even remember what he wanted to see me about. We got finished with our business. I had excused myself from my guests, and my wife was still there with them.

When I came back, one of the fellows, who was a professor at Hampton Institute, said, "George, do you go around with people like that?"

And I said, "If you all will excuse me, I want to tell all of you something. If I needed $100 tonight, I could get it from him. If I needed $100 tonight, I bet you I couldn't get it out of this whole damn room." I said, "That man is a friend of mine. He's as much a friend of mine as any one of you is. And he's as welcome in my home any time he wants to come here as any one of you is. I want you to never forget that." And you could hear a pin drop.

Q: I'll bet!

Mr. Cooper: You could hear a pin drop. And I was serious. I think I got that from Papa, too. I can remember Mama used to say, "Son, don't ever think you are smarter than anybody else, because nine times out of ten, the other person's got more sense than you ever thought you had." And there's a lot of truth in it, too. Don't ever think you're any better than anybody else. I don't know why I told you that story either.

Q: I think it's a good story.

Mr. Cooper: I don't know why I told you that one, but it has been a guiding factor in the life of this family. We see it in our daughter, Peggy Cooper Davis, for instance. She is a full professor with tenure at NYU after three and a half years.* We see it in her. We tried to instill it in this household. You're no better or no worse than anybody else in the world.

Q: How did the white chief petty officers relate to you?

Mr. Cooper: The interaction was with the black chiefs. There was not that much interaction with the white chiefs, because I don't think they wanted interaction. It was a little soon, it was a little new, it was a little too much for them.

Q: Were you accorded the authority of a chief petty officer?

Mr. Cooper: Oh, yes. Downes would see to that. No question about that. I had my family there, and we had our own quarters and everything, so we didn't have too much interaction that way in terms of living together. There was no chiefs' mess, for instance.

---
*NYU--New York University.

Q: Did you go through the traditional chiefs' initiation?

Mr. Cooper: No.

Q: That doesn't go to instant chiefs?

Mr. Cooper: That's right. That's right.

Q: What sort of a procedure went on at Great Lakes to make you a chief petty officer?

Mr. Cooper: Oh, I didn't go through anything. I just went up there and signed some papers.

Q: I see.

Mr. Cooper: I didn't go through any training. There was no training period.

Q: Did you make any conscious effort to learn more about the Navy?

Mr. Cooper: Not really, because I got a rate in the Navy, and I was going back to do the same job that I'd done before. I obviously had started, even as a civilian instructor, to learn a little about naval regulations and that kind of thing so that I could at least speak the language, but I put forth no special effort to learn about the Navy until I went into OCS, to be perfectly honest with you.*

Q: What about disciplinary situations? Did those come up while you were a chief at Hampton?

Mr. Cooper: Yes, but I didn't have any problems with them. You put a guy on report, and he's just on report. Discipline would come as a matter of course. I didn't have any particular problem with it.

Q: What this says, though, is you were more than just a classroom instructor. You had the traditional prerogatives of leading the men.

Mr. Cooper: Oh, yes.

Q: Did you see some men that you recognized as having greater potential, that you tried to encourage?

Mr. Cooper: No question about it, yes. And you did, in fact, encourage a few and influenced a few, but I think

---

*OCS--officer candidate school.

that's, again, a part of the game. That's what you're there for.

Q: You talked before about these various trips that you'd made, the one going up to Wilberforce to get that job, and back and forth between Hampton and Great Lakes. What kind of difficulties did you have in the traveling?

Mr. Cooper: Well, you'd obviously have difficulty traveling if you wanted to stop in a hotel or a motel. I can remember one trip that we took, for instance, between here and Hampton, where we were really tired. It was somewhere in the mountains of West Virginia. We stopped at a motel and asked for a room. They said they simply wouldn't accept us, but that there was a black man who lived down the road two or three miles. He had a house, and sometimes he took black people in, and his name was Cooper. We subsequently found Mr. Cooper and spent the night in his home. It was an interesting experience, because he said, "If you awaken during the middle of the night and somebody's trying to get in the window, it's my son. He frequently comes in that way if he comes home high. But he won't bother you." Fortunately, he didn't come home that night. But we had that kind of situation.

Early in our married life, when we took a trip, we would take our sandwiches with us, because we couldn't stop and buy hamburgers without going to the back door and having somebody hand them out to us. Rather than face that kind of situation, we simply took our lunch with us. You would plan a trip long ahead, far enough ahead so that you'd know where you'd be at dinner time and know where you were going to spend the night, and you'd write ahead or call ahead or do something so that you had that set up with a friend, so that you wouldn't have to have the embarrassment of being refused at a hotel or a motel. One learns how to survive when there's no alternative.

Q: Did you ever wind up sleeping in the car?

Mr. Cooper: Yes, if you don't know anybody in the area, you just pull on the side of the road and go to sleep. You'd be afraid to do that now, but you could do it then with reasonable safety. You did what you had to do.

Q: Would you describe Commander Downes from that period as a friend?

Mr. Cooper: Oh, yes. Yes, I considered him a friend of mine from the word go.

Q: What do you remember of the process by which you were selected to go to officer training?

Cooper #2 - 137

Mr. Cooper: I don't know. I have no recollection of that at all.

Q: What do you remember about being notified?

Mr. Cooper: Well, as I say, Downes did say to me, "You've got to go in the service. If you come in the Navy, we'll bring you in as a chief." He said that to me before I went in, and suggested, "If it's possible to go further, we'll see whatever we can do to enable you to progress as rapidly as you can, whenever anything like that is possible." But it was kept pretty much a secret--and, I think, by design--in terms of selecting these guys to go to Great Lakes, and they didn't want anybody to know about it. For that reason, I don't know what process they went through to do it, Downes or anybody else.

Q: Did he, for example, call you into his office and tell you that this was going to happen?

Mr. Cooper: No. He called me into his office and said, "You've got orders to go to Great Lakes, and I think you will not be sorry." That's about all he'd tell me.

Q: He didn't tell you at that point what the purpose was?

Mr. Cooper: No. We learned that when we got to Great Lakes. I suspected that that's what it was. Why the hell would he transfer me to Great Lakes? I didn't think they were transferring me to train metalsmiths at Great Lakes.

Q: Since you were pretty valuable to him, it would have to be something good for him to be willing to give you up.

Mr. Cooper: Yes. Of course, you recognize that, but you still didn't say, "This is what it is. This is what I'm going for," because you didn't know that.

Q: And you didn't feel like pressing him to ask.

Mr. Cooper: Hardly. No, even though you perceived him as a friend, you wouldn't do that.

Q: Jesse Arbor said that he didn't know for quite a long time why he was there. How soon did you realize, once you arrived at Great Lakes, that that's what this was?

Mr. Cooper: I don't really know, but my perception is that it could not have been that long, because we were there as a unit, and they couldn't have kept us there too long without beginning the training. And if they begin the training, they've got to say what the training's for. I don't recall that we stayed there any length of time before we knew what we were there for. The details escape me.

Q: Then your memory differs from Mr. Arbor's, because he said it was sort of, "These are things officers need to know," not that, "You are the people who are going to be the officers."

Mr. Cooper: If these are things that officers need to know, why the hell are you telling me about them?

Q: Were you given a series of tests upon arrival?

Mr. Cooper: I don't recall that we were. And Jesse may have a much better memory than I, and some of the other guys may have a better memory than mine.

Q: He's the only one who remembered it that way.

Mr. Cooper: My recollection is that we started classes shortly after we got there, and there would be no other reason to start classes, except that we were being trained to be officers.

Q: What do you remember of the living arrangement in the

barracks?

Mr. Cooper: It was strictly a barracks. The thing that I remember is that we did everything in the barracks except drill. If you had to go to sick bay, you obviously had to go out of the barracks. But we did all of our classroom work, all of our living, all of our everything right there in the barracks. As you are probably aware, Great Lakes had one of the biggest officer candidate training schools in the country, but ours was set up in the barracks as a completely segregated unit, and we did everything as a segregated unit.

Q: Now the drill you mentioned, what did that comprise?

Mr. Cooper: Pushing boots, or working with guys who were pushing boots.* That was a part of our training.

Q: Did your group itself march at all?

Mr. Cooper: I honestly don't remember. I recall helping people in boot camp push kids through boot camp. I recall that, but I don't recall us actually doing any drilling. I don't remember that.

---
*"Boot camp" is the Navy term for basic enlisted training. An individual recruit is known as a boot, and the process of leading the recruits through the training period is referred to as "pushing boots."

Q: Did you have any opportunities for physical training?

Mr. Cooper: We had calisthenics. That was a part of the training.

Q: Was that in the barracks?

Mr. Cooper: In the barracks. You did everything in the barracks!

Q: Did you have to clean up the barracks?

Mr. Cooper: I think we did. I don't remember any sailors coming in cleaning up after us.

Q: When I went through officer training, it was the same thing. The officer candidates cleaned, and the idea being that the inspector taught them standards of cleanliness by seeing how well they did.

Mr. Cooper: Yes, we must have done our own cleaning.

Q: Do you remember inspections?

Cooper #2 - 142

Mr. Cooper: So we had to do the cleaning. Now that you mention inspections, that's the only reason for inspections.

Q: What do you remember about keeping your uniforms in shape and personnel inspections?

Mr. Cooper: Well, I remember you better keep them in shape or you're going to be in trouble. And again, you see, like I've said a hundred times, not just to you, but to everybody with whom I've talked, we decided that we were going to sink or swim together, and keeping clean was one of the things that you had to do--uniform, body, and everything else. And that was a part of swimming and not sinking. If one of us got out of line, even in terms of a uniform being dirty or anything like that, the others would bring him right back in. We decided, "We've got to make this thing work." That thread went through everything we did.

Q: Was there a point that you stopped seeing yourselves as individuals, but rather as representatives of a much larger group, that you had to do well for all the blacks out there?

Mr. Cooper: I think we had that from the first, from the

very beginning.

Q: Was it something you talked about consciously?

Mr. Cooper: No question about it. Yes. And that was the basic part of the rationale for doing the thing together. We felt we had to win, because if we lost, if we failed, there were 120,000 men out there who wouldn't have a shot at this for a hell of a long time, probably.* It was an awesome responsibility. We talked about it constantly; we had to. And in a situation like that, each of us at some point in time got to the stage where he said, "The hell with it. This is just too damn much." And the others would have to be there to say, "Oh, no, man, we must do this."

Q: That's a lot of burden to bear.

Mr. Cooper: You better believe it. And each one of us, at one point in time or maybe more than one, got to the point where we were ready to throw in the towel, just too damn much, because we're human. But the others were always there.

Q: Were there leaders that developed in your group of 16?

―――――
*Life magazine, 24 April 1944, page 44, indicated that there were 120,000 blacks in the Navy at the time.

Mr. Cooper: I think Baugh turned out to be a leader in the group, and in his own way, Jess Arbor. Again, in a different kind of way, Phil Barnes, the fat guy.

Q: In what way did each of these demonstrate his leadership?

Mr. Cooper: You can ask the most piercing questions. Jess would sense something going wrong, for instance, and Jess can reach and pull a joke out of the air at the drop of a hat. He's got one for almost every kind of a situation you can imagine. He would say something that would just clear the air and just sort of soothe the thing over to make you, as a result of laughing at one of his stupid jokes, stop and think, if you will.

Baugh was a much more serious-minded person, and he took the position, "Oh, man, just stop this crap. We just can't do this," you know, that kind of thing.

Phil Barnes was a guy who would have been a gospel singer. That may not mean anything to you, but Phil would take that perspective on the thing and say, "You know, it's just wrong for us to do this. It's wrong for us to go this way, morally wrong. We just can't afford to do it."

So that in different ways, one of us would come

forward at the appropriate time and say, "No. Hold it. Hold it. We can't do it. Straighten it up."

Q: Were you a leader in the group also?

Mr. Cooper: I suppose there were times when it was my turn, either on my own or in support of another, to lead. The situation demanded constant vigilance, vision, courage, strength, and faith. Each of us led at some point.

Q: Who came up with this idea of working together?

Mr. Cooper: I don't know. I honestly don't know. I suspect it just grew out of the group. You know, here were a bunch of guys, most of whom had never seen each other before, and you're put in a situation where you're representing, each of you, thousands of people, the 16 of us and 120,000 servicemen. Nobody has to tell you that you've got to stick together. You've just got to do it. I don't think anybody laid it on the table and said, "This is what we've got to do." It just evolved.

Q: Well, I think camaraderie is bound to develop in any kind of situation like that. People have to submerge their individualities sometimes for the common good.

Mr. Cooper: Yes.

Q: What sorts of things were covered in the training?

Mr. Cooper: What do you mean, what sorts of things?

Q: The curriculum, the subject matter?

Mr. Cooper: Navigation, aircraft and warship identification, law, the normal things studied by any officer candidate. We had the same curriculum the other candidates had.

Q: You couldn't have much seamanship there in the barracks.

Mr. Cooper: We did. Now, that's where Jess excelled, particularly as it related to identification and signalling. He would lead us through that stuff, and he'd pick it up just like that. (snaps fingers)

Q: It sounds as if a lot of it was rote memory work.

Mr. Cooper: It was. No question about it.

Q: You learned a lot of information.

Mr. Cooper: In a hurry. That's where the drills in the head after lights-out would come into play. We'd sit there and drill each other until we were ready for class the next day.

Q: You said before, and didn't really amplify it, that you didn't perceive that the Navy was making a completely good-faith effort in this. Why not?

Mr. Cooper: It was partially demonstrated by the quality and the character of the people they gave us as instructors. I think that was probably my rationale in terms of making that statement. And I've thought about that since our first interview. I suspect that the Navy, as an institution, was serious about it, because the President had ordered it. The President had, in fact, ordered it, you see. But the people who were selected to instruct us were individuals; they were not the institution. And they brought their prejudices with them, so that from that perspective, by design, they tried to make us fail.

Now, another real consideration is when our grades were sent up and we were higher than any other indoctrination class, again, I don't think the institution said, "Send them back through it again because somebody made a mistake." I think that was an individual response, if that makes any sense to you.

Q: Did you repeat the whole curriculum?

Mr. Cooper: No. They immediately discovered that this was a mistake. You know, the guys will do better than ever if you send them back through the same thing again! We didn't go back through it.

Q: One idea that challenges your notion that it wasn't a good-faith effort is that the people such as you who were picked, were people who were capable of doing it.

Mr. Cooper: They could have picked real duds.

Q: And said, "See, it didn't work."

Mr. Cooper: They could have done that. That's the reason I say I don't think the institution as an entity operated in bad faith. There are people in institutions, and people impact on institutions.

Q: Commander Downes was one of the people in that institution. It was obviously good faith on his part.

Cooper #2 - 149

Mr. Cooper: No question about it. Jack Dille is another one. Lieutenant Paul Richmond was another one, and Graham Martin, I think, can tell you about Richmond when you see him.*

Q: You mentioned, before we started the tape, an instructor that you especially remembered. What was it about him that sticks in your mind?

Mr. Cooper: His name was Lou Heitger.** He was not one of our instructors; he was a fellow officer at Hampton. And Lou died, I suppose 15 years ago. He was from Indiana. He was one of the most compassionate and caring human beings I've ever seen in my life. Lou became a very good friend, and we stayed friends until he died. If he wasn't a Quaker, he should have been one.

Q: You mentioned that there were some instructors who weren't all that great. Were there some who were sympathetic and encouraging?

Mr. Cooper: Richmond was encouraging. Jack Dille, obviously, was the one who was most encouraging and most supportive and most helpful. We had a black instructor

---
*Lieutenant Paul D. Richmond, USNR, was navigation instructor for the group.
**Lieutenant Louis C. Heitger, USNR.

named Noble Payton who obviously was supportive, because he was one of us.*

Q: Were the instructors predominantly white?

Mr. Cooper: Predominantly white, 80%-plus white. And officers.

Q: Were they knowledgeable in their subject matter?

Mr. Cooper: Oh, I think reasonably so, yes. I don't think they sent duds in to teach us. They sent people who were, I think, qualified to teach, but who had their own private and individual prejudices.

Q: So it was more a matter of attitude.

Mr. Cooper: More a matter of attitude than subject matter, yes.

Q: How would you describe the routine in a typical day while you were undergoing the training?

Mr. Cooper: The bugle sounds, and you get your butt out of bed, have calisthenics. Normal routine. An hour later, you start your classes, break for lunch, just do a regular

---

*Noble Payton was a chemist who during the course of his career taught at several colleges, including Bethune-Cookman College and Howard University.

routine day.*

Q: You went to another building for meals, didn't you?

Mr. Cooper: Yes. We had to go to the mess hall for meals, and there again we were set off in a little area, as I recall.

Q: Apart from the black enlisted people.

Mr. Cooper: Yes.

Q: Did there seem to be a conscious effort to keep information from leaking out about what was going on?

Mr. Cooper: There's no question about it. Yes. It was a secret. And I suppose reasonably so. They really didn't know whether it was going to work or not. As you suggest, even though they felt that they had a handpicked group of people, they didn't really know whether it was going to work or not, because it never happened before.

Q: Well, we've said they obviously didn't pick duds. But, on the other hand, they got guys who didn't all have college. There was a spectrum of experience there. The

---
*A copy of a sample week's schedule is included with this volume as an appendix.

Navy might have hedged the bets more by, say, getting people, all who had master's degrees, which certainly would have been possible.

Mr. Cooper: It's possible. But, again, I think that the institution was smart enough to say, "We want a variety here." And the institution, I believe, wanted to give it an honest shot.

Q: It wouldn't have proved the point as well if you all had master's degrees.

Mr. Cooper: Exactly.

Q: What sorts of hazing did you undergo during that period?

Mr. Cooper: We didn't have any hazing. We were there together.

Q: No, I mean, was there any hazing of your group by those who were not members of the group?

Mr. Cooper: There was nobody there who wasn't a member of the group, but the instructors.

Q: Were they, in any cases, demeaning?

Mr. Cooper: I don't recall that, no. They were tough and hard as instructors, but there was no hazing, as I recall.

Q: How was their prejudice manifested?

Mr. Cooper: I suppose--and this is a sincere answer--that you'd have to be black to really appreciate it. Prejudice is exerted in so many subtle and unobvious ways that a black person senses it and smells it and feels it. It's in a glance, it's in the tone of voice, it's in an attitude, which if you've never been exposed to it, you just won't catch. Does that make sense to you?* There are so many subtle ways of demonstrating prejudice, but as a black person, you just have antennas out, and you sense it and you feel it instinctively.

Q: I will appreciate whatever efforts you can make to verbalize it for those who might read this or hear the tape.

Mr. Cooper: A demeaning attitude can be exemplified in such subtle ways that, except that you have your antenna

---

*This question was addressed to Ms. NeAnni Ife, a friend of Mr. Cooper, who sat in and listened to a portion of the interview.

out, you'd never know it was there. A request can be made of you to do this, that, or the other, and the mere tone of voice and the approach that that person takes in making that request is demeaning, suggests a sense of superiority and inferiority. And it's so frequently done by people who, if you're on the bitter end of it, are so much your inferior in so many ways until it takes a hell of a lot of guts to even stomach it. And you know this and you sense this and you feel this, and it takes me back to what Mama used to say, "Son, it ain't no sin being colored, but it's darned inconvenient."

Q: You might perceive it also in a lack of enthusiasm, that the person would go through the motions and follow orders.

Mr. Cooper: Yes, that, too. The kind of thing that you would never see in a Jack Dille, for instance, because Jack would display the kind of enthusiasm that you allude to, and you'd know immediately that here's a sincere human being. You could sense that, too.

Q: I would like to get a better handle on what he did for the group, what he did with the group.

Mr. Cooper: Well, you've talked with him.

Q: I've talked with him. But how do you perceive it?

Mr. Cooper: I don't really know how to express it, except to say that Jack Dille, in my judgment, is a decent, honorable, caring human being, and Jack has enough to bury all of us in money. He obviously doesn't do this for any personal gain in terms of his relationship with us as members of the Golden Thirteen; he does it because he wants to do it. He does it because he thinks that it's an honor for us to consider him one of us, and I think he honestly believes that. And he does that because he's, in my judgment, an unusual person. I don't know what makes Jack tick. I do know that many years ago Jack was partially responsible for the creation of an entity called Broadcap and served as its first president. The agency was created for the purpose of and continues to provide financial assistance to minorities in the ownership and operation of radio and TV stations. When he left our recent reunion in Atlanta, he was going to a board meeting the next day, and I forget how many millions of dollars they have in that entity now, to help blacks get into the ownership end of the media business. And Jack started this thing. He's made it go. I mean, he's been the driving force behind it. He's just a good man.*

---
*John F. Dille, Jr., is chairman of Federated Media, which has both newspaper and broadcast holdings. Dille attends

Cooper #2 - 156

Q: One thing I can imagine him doing for you back then is giving you faith in yourselves.

Mr. Cooper: He was always there when you needed him, and you knew he was there.

Q: Could you confide in him?

Mr. Cooper: Yes. And Jack would go to bat for you, to the extent that he felt that he could as an officer in the Navy. He'd go to bat for you, even beyond that, a little beyond it. I can't recall the details, but I sense that there were times when I felt that Jack might have bent over a little bit too far in terms of possibly hurting himself to try to support us. And I don't remember the details.

Q: He had one big asset in that regard, in that he was not a career Navy man.

Mr. Cooper: He wasn't career, that's right.

Q: So he could afford to take that risk.

---

Golden Thirteen reunions and is listed, along with the 13 officers, on the Golden Thirteen's stationery.

Mr. Cooper: Yes, but he didn't have to do it. Even as a non-career man, he didn't have to do it, but he did it. And that means a lot to us and always will.

Q: Do you remember any specifics where he went to bat for you?

Mr. Cooper: I suspect Jess might. I don't remember.

Q: Arbor said that he wished I'd come around years earlier, because he may not be remembering it exactly anymore; he may remember some things that didn't happen.

Mr. Cooper: Jess has a good memory.

Q: What do you remember about the off-duty time in the barracks? How did you spend that?

Mr. Cooper: I suspect playing cards occasionally to lighten the load. I don't, for instance, recall partying per se, even going out when we had liberty. And, again, you know, we weren't kids when we went into this thing; we were pretty serious and we were pretty adult people. And we knew that we were in a situation that was going to require everything we had to put into it, and we didn't do too much partying.

Q: But you've got to have some form of relaxation, just to keep your perspective.

Mr. Cooper: We used to play cards as a group together, and then you'd have liberty, and you'd go out. There were times when I'd go home to see my family two or three times while we were there, and the guys would go into Chicago. Dennis Nelson would ride around in his car, and some of the guys would ride with him. But we didn't do too much partying.

Q: There were probably also times when you got on each other's nerves. How did you deal with those occasions?

Mr. Cooper: Jesse Arbor. Jesse and Phil Barnes. There were a lot of times when you'd get on each other's nerves. You had to in a tight living situation like that.

Q: Especially with all that pressure.

Mr. Cooper: And, again, you know, you've got to take your hat off to Jess; he'd come through.

Q: How would he deal with it--with the light words or mediate?

Mr. Cooper: I'll tell you, Jess could reach back and pull a joke out of the hat for any situation that came down the pike. He's had a knack for doing it, and he was a tremendous influence on that group.

Q: This working together that you did, did you keep the knowledge of that from the instructors?

Mr. Cooper: Well, we didn't advertise the fact that we studied in the head after lights-out. We certainly didn't do that. I don't know that there was any conscious effort put forth to say, "We're together," or "We're not together." I think it was obvious that we were together.

Q: Well, it was tolerated, then, by those in charge.

Mr. Cooper: There's nothing you can do about it. What could you do about it? If you want to be together, you're going to be together.

Q: I suppose you could put some sort of a monitor in or what have you, some duty officer.

Mr. Cooper: There was never any of that kind of thing.

Q: You talked about the professional subjects like

navigation and recognition and so forth. Was there any training in how to be an officer, the things that officers do, the things they say?

Mr. Cooper: I forget what they called the course. Yes. We had weekly sheets, you know, and I still have some of them around here somewhere.*

Q: If you could find those, that would be great for the record.

Mr. Cooper: I think so. I think we can come up with something.

Q: What more can you say about the role of Commander Armstrong?

Mr. Cooper: Well, he was in command of the whole Great Lakes, or the whole base, but we didn't really have that much interaction with him.

Q: Was he just Camp Robert Smalls?

Mr. Cooper: No, he was on the main side.

---
*Some of Mr. Cooper's course materials are included as an appendix to this volume.

Cooper #2 - 161

Q: I see.

Mr. Cooper: Armstrong was on the main side. Robert Smalls was under his jurisdiction, part of his command, so that we didn't really have any interaction with him, except when we had our final interviews.

Q: How would you compare him as a leader with Downes?

Mr. Cooper: Of course, we were never exposed to Armstrong like we were to Downes. You know, you never get to the top man in a command that big, that massive.

Q: Were there intermediate officers that you had more contact with?

Mr. Cooper: There's no question about it, yes.

Q: Who were some of those?

Mr. Cooper: Well, all of the officers who served as our instructors, such as Lieutenant (j.g.) Headley, Ensign Lowry, and Lieutenant Quattlebaum.* And I would assume--

---

*Lieutenant (junior grade) F. G. Headley, USNR, was the seamanship instructor; Ensign J. W. Lowry, USNR, was the Navy Regulations instructor; Lieutenant W. I. Quattlebaum, USN (Ret.), was the gunnery instructor. Outlines for these courses are in an appendix at the end of the volume.

and I don't even recall the details of this--there was somebody who acted as a liaison person between this group and the main side. I don't remember who that person would have been, who would have been sort of an overseer for the school, somebody in charge.

Q: I think Goodwin had something of a liaison role. How would you describe that?

Mr. Cooper: Well, Goodwin had obviously been at Great Lakes and had developed a relationship, not just with the people at Camp Robert Smalls, but with Armstrong himself, and served as sort of a liaison person between the group and him simply because he knew Goodwin, knew him personally, and Goodwin knew Armstrong personally. I don't think that there was any official liaison set up between main side and Goodwin. I think it was unofficial.

Q: Were there situations, say, where your group had a concern or a grievance or whatever, that Goodwin could go and voice it with Commander Armstrong?

Mr. Cooper: There would be concerns where Goodwin would go and voice it to somebody. Goodwin was not an outgoing kind of person, and you frequently didn't know what Goodwin was thinking.

Q: Did you get answers to these concerns?

Mr. Cooper: Yes. Yes, he'd come back with answers on occasions, and sometimes he'd come back and he didn't have the answers. I think he performed that function well.

Q: Would it have been more difficult for you as a group if there had not been somebody in Goodwin's role?

Mr. Cooper: I think so, yes. I think so.

Q: Are there any specifics that you recall about issues that he did take to the front office?

Mr. Cooper: No, and I realize you're pushing for specifics.

Q: They help.

Mr. Cooper: Because it will help you in your writing. But my God, that's been 45 years ago, and a lot of water's gone over the dam in 45 years.

Q: You mentioned the investigation had turned up this

Cooper #2 - 164

squabble you'd had as an eight-year-old.  Did you have any other evidence of how thorough the investigation was on you?

Mr. Cooper:  I subsequently ran into people, both at Hampton Institute, where I had worked as a civilian and had gone to school, and even in the little town of Washington, North Carolina, where people had gone and checked.  People had gone and asked about me and that kind of thing, FBI, obviously.  They did a pretty thorough check on each of us.

Q:  I can see a reason for that is to avoid embarrassments. I think you can put a positive connotation on that, that the Navy wanted to make sure it was getting good people for this experiment.

Mr. Cooper:  Yes.  I follow your logic, obviously.  An impertinent response is they didn't do it to you.

Q:  They did do it to me.

Mr. Cooper:  The same thing?  I wonder if they did it to you to the extent that they did it to us.  I really do.

Q:  They sent the FBI out.

Cooper #2 - 165

Mr. Cooper: There's an awful lot of officers in the Navy.

Q: For a security clearance, they certainly checked me out.

Mr. Cooper: Well, but that was after you had become an officer and needed a security clearance.

Q: Yes.

Mr. Cooper: That wasn't when you went in as a young officer, as a prerequisite for being made an officer, being commissioned.

Q: I don't remember how much checking they did before.

Mr. Cooper: I doubt that very seriously. But for clearance, certainly. And I may be wrong. It's just an impression that I have.

Q: Did you resent that it had been done?

Mr. Cooper: Yes. Yes. Because, again, I felt that it was not the usual thing. It was not par for the course. On the other hand, I say to you it may have been par for the course and I was not aware of it, but I did resent it

Cooper #2 - 166

because I thought it was not par for the course. Just as I still resent being put to test for no other reason than the fact that I'm a different color.

Q: I can understand that.

Mr. Cooper: And it happens still today. So that I think it's a normal resentment, natural.

Q: We talked before about the role that Phil Barnes's sister played. What specific kinds of things can you recall?

Mr. Cooper: Details I simply can't recall, but she was in an office situation in Washington, which gave her access to certain kinds of intelligence, which, as I recall, was subsequently fed back to us, the details of which I don't recall at all.

Q: But it was apparently useful to you.

Mr. Cooper: Yes. And as I recall, always positive, you know, not negative. Positive.

Q: Did your families help in providing this support, as well as the members of the group itself?

Mr. Cooper: Your families had to. When you're in any stressful situation, you obviously turn first to family, simply because it's a natural thing to do. Any accomplishment, if I can claim any, has to do with my wife and the support that I've gotten from her, including this obviously. You call on the telephone and just cry your heart out, and there's somebody on the other end of the line who's going to listen to you and she's going to say, "Keep your chin up."

Q: Did you have the feeling that there were any Navy chaplains at Great Lakes that you could go to for help?

Mr. Cooper: No. No. Well, in the first place, I hadn't been there. I didn't know anybody in Great Lakes. Goodwin and, I think, White or maybe Barnes, who had been there, might have done that, but I didn't.

Q: So you were almost exclusively left to your own resources.

Mr. Cooper: Yes.

Q: You told the story before about Commander Armstrong confronting you as a troublemaker. What else do you remember about the period of actually getting commissioned?

Mr. Cooper: Well, after that little incident, I was dismissed, and there was no conclusion. Then somebody else came in and read something to us which said, "You're a commissioned officer," and handed it to us. He didn't do it.

Q: Did it happen as a group?

Mr. Cooper: No, it happened individually. We were called in one by one. We had no graduation exercise; there was no fanfare at all. We were just handed a piece of paper that said, "You are now an officer and a gentleman."

Q: What were your emotional responses to that experience?

Mr. Cooper: It's hard to say. I think each of us recognized that we'd gone through hell to get there. I think also that each of us recognized that having gone through that hell, we may have laid the seed, the groundwork, for somebody else to come along and do the same thing, and to, in fact, become an officer in the United States Navy. So that you had a sense of relief, a sense of pride, a sense of accomplishment, all of which I think was natural.

Q: Elation?

Mr. Cooper: Yes. I think obvious elation.

Q: Did you have any contact with the three men who didn't make it?

Mr. Cooper: None. By design, I'm sure. I'm sure by design.

Q: You mentioned one that you didn't feel was up to it from the standpoint of ability. Who was that?

Mr. Cooper: Lear, the guy who committed suicide.

Q: But he made it, though. I mean, he wasn't one of the three.

Mr. Cooper: He made warrant officer. Oh, no, he was not one of the three who was put out, who did not make it at all. Lear was made warrant officer.

The three who didn't make it, I think, were capable of making it. I'm sure they had what it took to do it intellectually. There were some other reasons they were snatched out of it. I don't know what those reasons were.

Cooper #2 - 170

We were talking about it, as a matter of fact, two weeks ago at our reunion in Atlanta. We never really knew what happened to any of the three of them. I didn't, at least. I don't think any of the rest of the guys did.

Q: Did you have any perception that those three had done less well than the 13 who made it?

Mr. Cooper: No, I don't. There was some external force there, I'm almost positive of that, something outside the group, something outside the intellectual ability or the ability to go through the process, something beyond that.

Q: And I think you're also saying something beyond what they achieved in the group, too.

Mr. Cooper: Yes.

Mr. Cooper: I showed you a book before the interview started which made the assertion that the Navy arbitrarily decided that not all the men in your training course would be commissioned.*

Mr. Cooper: That's one man's opinion. I don't know the answer to that.

Q: We talked about the various individuals before who were commissioned. I wonder if you have any individual recollections on the other three: Williams, Alves, and Pinkney.

Mr. Cooper: As I recall, Pinkney was a hail fellow, well met type, like Arbor. Alves was, as I recall, more like Goodwin. That's as far as I can go.

Q: You don't remember Williams specifically?

Mr. Cooper: Mummy. I have less recollection of Mummy than any of the rest of them, I really do, despite the fact that I've gotten to know him since then. As you know, he is still in Chicago.

---

*Bernard C. Nalty, Strength for the Fight (New York: The Free Press, 1986), makes the following statement on page 192: ". . .on January 1, 1944, sixteen black enlisted men entered a segregated officer candidate school at the Great Lakes Naval Training Station. Although all of them successfully completed the course, only twelve received commissions, a purely arbitrary number adopted by the Bureau of Personnel for reasons never explained. Of the remaining four, one became a warrant officer, and the others reverted to enlisted status."

Q: In fact, I'm going to see him in a few days. I'm, again, searching for any other specific incidents that you recall from that training period that would be useful to put on the record.

Mr. Cooper: I think you've about pumped me dry.

Q: It sounds as if there were not any great watershed events; it was one day after another.

Mr. Cooper: One day at a time. I think it had to be that way, really, because you never knew from one day to the next what was going to come up and what you were going to have to be confronted with, so you took it one day at a time. You were plowing new ground. And I really think that that's the underlying consideration--that we recognized that we were plowing new ground. We came to the realization that it had to be done as well as we could do it. And no matter what happened the next day, you'd have to face that and do it as well as you knew to respond to it, to the best of your ability, no matter what it was.

Q: Could you, at the time, realize the historic importance of this achievement?

Mr. Cooper: I doubt it. We say each of us represented so many thousand sailors simply by virtue of the number of blacks. The significance of the thing, I don't think, hit us. It didn't hit me to the fullest extent, the extent that you recognize now.

Q: You described the situation at the Chicago railroad station, where your appearance stopped traffic. Were there other experiences like that for you?

Mr. Cooper: Yes. People would just stop. Things would stop on the street. When I went back to Hampton, I was the only black officer in a radius of 500 miles, and obviously a new entity. But you run across that all the time in the service and out of the service, everywhere you went. There's no such thing as a black naval officer. There isn't one.

Q: You talked about the one fellow that you almost came to blows with. Were there any positive experiences of people recognizing you?

Mr. Cooper: Yes. Oh, yes. There were a number of guys, for instance, in ship's company especially, and some in the officers' rank who, in my judgment, went out of their way to try to be supportive. There's good and bad in every situation.

Q: Did you take any disciplinary action against people who did not accord you the respect due an officer?

Mr. Cooper: No. The answer to that is clearly no. I'd find a way to work around him. I alluded to that in the last interview. I'd find a way to get him to come by me as an officer, because the idea was to win him over, rather than try to kick him in the butt.

Q: What did your job responsibilities include as personnel officer?

Mr. Cooper: Well, the usual duties of a personnel officer, overseeing leave and that kind of thing, liberty. The way you'd get a guy in was that if a guy needed to go home--for instance, on emergency leave--I used that frequently. With the ship's company, there was always somebody who had some sort of emergency situation we had to respond to. Or, if not that, you'd find some other personnel angle from which you could work, so that you'd have an opportunity to interact with him, and you tried your damndest to make that person respect you as a human being, as opposed to trying to force him to respect you, simply by virtue of the fact that you wore a uniform. You could have done that. It's an accepted part of military operations: "You don't respect me, respect the uniform." That doesn't win friends and influence people. In my judgment, it doesn't. And nobody ever said you had to do that.

Q: There must have been some aspects of the job other than gaining respect, the mundane things like dealing with paperwork and what have you. What was involved in those things?

Mr. Cooper: I don't understand what you're saying, what you're asking.

Q: Well, you've described that a by-product of your job was getting the people in and dealing with them so they recognized you as a human. But that's a by-product. There's a main job which consists of administering personnel.

Mr. Cooper: You obviously do that. That's your job.

Q: I'm trying to see if you remember any specifics about that phase of it. Did you have, say, a group of yeomen working for you that worked on service records, training records?

Cooper #2 - 176

Mr. Cooper: Sure. Sure. The normal thing, yes. You supervised that help just like you would in a civilian situation. I don't recall that I had any difficulty in that area, because, again, it's like the young woman I alluded to in the first part of the interview. You command respect or you don't.

Q: The respect you earn is much more genuine than that which you browbeat into people.

Mr. Cooper: I think so. I think so.

Q: Was there any sense of disappointment that you experienced when this physical situation led you to getting out of the Navy, rather than going overseas?

Mr. Cooper: I sort of looked forward to going overseas, because I felt that I wanted that experience, that exposure. So that when I found out that I did have this physical problem, it was something of a disappointment. I must be honest enough to say it didn't last too long, because after the initial disappointment, I was able to stay with my family, and that was a real pleasure for me.

Q: Sure.

Mr. Cooper: I didn't have to leave my family. And, as I say, I never thought that I was cut out to be a military man anyway.

Q: How large a role would you say that patriotism played as a motivator for the Golden Thirteen?

Mr. Cooper: I think as much as any black person, if that makes sense to you. I think we had that kind of motivation as much as any sailor or any soldier who's black. Who was it who said that, "Our battle for democracy will begin when we reach San Francisco on our way back home"? Recognizing that you do what you have to do, and you recognize that in spite of everything, this is the best country we know, so there is an element of patriotism that I think is very real.

Q: I remember quite vividly that movie A Soldier's Story, where the main thing that those black soldiers wanted was a chance to go fight for their country.*

Mr. Cooper: You recall the responses of skippers when we came back from the Civil War and they had black soldiers and sailors working under them, who felt they were the best

---

*This 1984 feature film dealt with the racial tensions produced in a southern Army camp in World War II when a black sergeant was murdered under mysterious circumstances.

Cooper #2 - 178

going. They were some of their best men. Because, again, this was better than anything else we knew, or better than anything else we know, even today.

Q: What did your work consist of with the veterans after you left the Navy?

Mr. Cooper: I was in charge of veterans' programs at Hampton Institute back in Tidewater, Virginia, and you had all these people coming out on the GI Bill and going to school, and they needed debriefing and all kinds of things.* That was an interesting experience, a learning experience for me, and, again, one which I wonder sometimes I didn't get more out of it than they got out of it, because you're exposed to so much and you learn so much in the process of trying to respond to the needs of people.

Q: One of the reasons for having this second interview is to bring us up to date on your connections with the Navy. Was there a long void there after you left the service?

Mr. Cooper: Yes, a void until Nelson was successful in getting the Navy to pull us back together in San Francisco. During that period of time, we had literally lost touch

---

*The GI Bill was a post-World War II program in which the U. S. Government paid college tuition for veterans of the war.

with each other, most of us had, except Jess and Syl White.

Q: Did you carry a positive feeling for the service during those years?

Mr. Cooper: I would say so. Because even though you weren't actively involved in it, you obviously kept up with current events and you would see progress being made in terms of upward mobility on the part of blacks in the service, in the Navy, as well as in the other branches of the service. You had positive feelings about that.

Q: Was it during that time that your realization grew of your own role in that progress?

Mr. Cooper: Probably, but I suspect unconsciously.

Q: Made much more overt then after Nelson got the group together. What kinds of things have you done since then as a group and individually for the Navy?

Mr. Cooper: I can speak more in terms of individually than as a group, because each of us is doing his own thing, obviously. In Dayton, I've become very active with the Navy League. I've put forth some effort to try to get blacks into the junior ROTC program. We got a Sea Cadet program set up in a black high school here, and I had something to do with that. I served as the first black president of the local chapter of the Navy League, during which time I developed and got approved by our board of directors some rather positive things related to blacks in the service and increased support for the Sea Cadet program in Dayton.

I've worked in recruitment and rather closely with the campus liaison officer at Central State University, Joe Lewis.* Dr. Lewis is, in my judgment, one of the best CLOs we have in the service, one of the most sincere and hard working. We worked rather closely with him.

In addition to that, I have worked with local recruiters, principally Glen Witt.** If you interview him, he will tell you of some of the things that we did together, which I think you might find interesting for the record. It was he, obviously, who was responsible for us being invited to go to Holy Loch.

Q: How did that come about? Did he just call up and say, "Do you want to go to Holy Loch?" Or what sorts of spadework did he do?

Mr. Cooper: Glen was working with young blacks on the
___
*Captain Joseph D. Lewis, USNR, of Central State University, Wilberforce, Ohio, about 15 miles east of Dayton.
**FTBC (SS) Glen Witt, USN.

ship, the Simon Lake.*

Q: Had he served in that ship himself?

Mr. Cooper: He was on the ship as a chief petty officer. He'd been working to help develop programs for Black History Month. He said to the group, in one of the sessions that they had, "I know a member of the Golden Thirteen, and maybe that would be a good thing to do, to try to get him over here and sort of culminate our celebration of Black History Month."

Some of the men from his ship said, "Who is the Golden Thirteen?" And he told them. These young sailors said, "When did this happen?"

He said, "1944."

One of them said, "Well, if you know him, you'd better get him on the phone and bring him over here, because he might not be long for this world."

And that very evening, Glen called. Peg answered the phone. He said he wanted to speak to me, and she said, "Well, he's not here, but he will call you back. If you give me a number, Glen, he will call you back. Where are you calling from?"

He said, "I'm calling from Scotland."

---
*The USS Simon Lake (AS-33) is a submarine tender equipped to provide maintenance and supply support to deployed ballistic missile submarines when they are between deterrent patrols.

"Scotland, Tennessee?"

He said, "No, Scotland, Scotland, over in Europe."

She said, "I don't think he'll call you back then, but he'll be home in about an hour."

And he called me back in an hour and wanted to know if I'd come over. I discovered that these young fellows working with Glen and with a black master chief, when they decided they wanted to bring me over, went to the command of the ship and said, "We need some help financially for this thing. We'd like to do it." And as I understand it, the response was, "Well, we could probably do it next year. We're halfway through the month now. It's pretty late to try to get something done and do it timely in terms of B Black History Month." And that very evening, they passed the hat and raised $3,000.

Q: In the ship's crew?

Mr. Cooper: In the ship's crew. Then the command did, in fact, throw some money in the pot. I told them to send two tickets, and I'd reimburse them for my wife's ticket, because obviously they had no obligation to pay for her. They met us and took us to this two-bedroom chalet which they had rented for us, completely stocked. We had a car and a driver from the Marine contingent on the ship. The red carpet was rolled out. I think it's undoubtedly the best trip we've ever made, and we've done a fair amount of traveling. It was the best trip, in my judgment, by virtue of the opportunity the trip afforded us to interact with these young blacks on the ship, in terms of trying to help them get the most out of the experience.

What we saw was a group of young people, 18, 19, 20, 21, 22 years old, doing their job in the Navy and doing it well, and doing all kinds of things, but needing a push to take full advantage of being in a foreign land, needing a push to take full advantage of upward mobility opportunities in the Navy itself, and needing some old folks just to talk to. Indeed, before we left, Peg and I said, "You know, if you raise enough money to pay the rent on this chalet, we'll just stay over here and be Mom and Papa for the whole ship."

Interestingly enough, we had interaction, in my judgment, which was positive, not just with the black crew members aboard that ship, but with the whole ship--from the command structure down. We made some real friends on that trip, and we will be very, very disappointed if we don't see people stop by here periodically and consider this as their second home.

Q: When did that trip take place?

Mr. Cooper: The end of February, first week in March.

Black History Month, the end of February.

Q: You mentioned before the tape started a touching incident during the trip.

Mr. Cooper: Yes. We were having chow one day in the crew's mess, and a young black chief from one of the subs--and I didn't know who he was--just came up and introduced himself, wanted to meet us as a member of the Golden Thirteen. He wanted to know if we would do him a favor. And I said, "Well, of course--whatever you think we can do, we'll be glad to do it."

And he said, "It would honor me if you would wear this." And he reached up and took his dolphins, and wanted me to have them.* And, of course, I accepted them as graciously as I knew how. But poor, dumb me did not realize the significance of that act on his part until Chief Witt explained it afterwards. By this time, the young man's sub had left, and we didn't know how to find him, didn't know his name or anything. Chief Witt finally got his name, rank, and serial number so we could write to him.

Q: What did Witt say was the significance of the gesture?

---
*Qualified submariners, both officer and enlisted, wear a metal breast insignia on their uniforms. Two dolphins are featured in the insignia.

Mr. Cooper: This was his initial set of dolphins, and your original set, they either put them on you when you die, or when you die they send them home to your mother. And that was quite a moving experience for us, to have somebody like that.

Another interesting thing that happened--one of the subs that was in when we were there was the George Washington Carver.* Peg and I got a chance to go aboard, and that was quite an experience, too.

Q: There was another story you told me before the tape started that I would like to get on the record, please, and that's about the people that you inspired to be officers.

Mr. Cooper: Oh, yes. The kids tried to make it so that it was not all work and no play. They gave parties for us and took us on trips. We went, for instance--two stories, if I may.

Q: Tell all you like.

Mr. Cooper: We were on our way to Edinburgh, actually to go to a museum and to do some touring, but principally to

---

*The USS George Washington Carver (SSBN-656) is a nuclear-powered ballistic missile submarine named for the noted black scientist and inventor who developed many useful products from the peanut and sweet potato.

go to a museum to see this Egyptian show. On the way there, we had some of the fellows with us, and one of them said, "Mr. Cooper, as a result of you and Mrs. Cooper being here, four of us have decided to try for officers." The young white Marine driver said, "And two of us, because I'm one of them." And we felt that the trip was worth that, if nothing else happened.

But the interesting story about the museum was that we had gone one day earlier and wanted to see the show the day it opened, and there were lines three and four blocks long. We simply couldn't get in, because we didn't have time to stand in line. Somebody from the base wrote a letter. We went the second time. We had a copy of this letter in our hands saying that these people were VIPs and guests of the United States Navy, that in addition to that, they were both in their 70s, and they couldn't stand in line, and "Would you please see if you can assist them?" We walked in front of 300 waiting people and got a chance to see this exhibit. We had that kind of support from the command structure.

They entertained us, showed us a good time. As a matter of fact, at one point we had to say to the brass, "We have to spend more time with the kids, because they sent for us and they paid for it. We appreciate what you're willing to do for us, but we came over for another purpose." And they appreciated that, too. As a matter of fact, in our meeting in Atlanta just last week, I laid this on the table as an agenda item--the fact that members of the Golden Thirteen individually could do this sort of thing anywhere in the world at very little expense to the Navy. And I felt that the results of it would be worth infinitely more than the cost.

Q: How had you gotten to know Chief Witt before the phone call from Scotland?

Mr. Cooper: He and I worked very closely together when he was in Navy recruiting here in Dayton.

Q: What other things did you do as Navy League president besides the work on the Sea Cadet program?

Mr. Cooper: One of the things I did was bring two or three other blacks into the Navy League as members, and we're still trying to do that, as well as getting any new member in. I'm currently working on a ways and means committee to see what we can do to raise additional money so we can give a little bit better and more support to the Sea Cadet program in Dayton, to enlarge and make it bigger and better.

I work tangentially with a program committee to try to

bring the right kinds of programs to the Navy League. As a result of having been in Atlanta, just in a meeting day before yesterday, I laid three names on the table of people that I thought would be willing to come, because I had spoken to them in Atlanta. One in particular I thought we could have come in for one of our meetings and sponsor people from Dr. Lewis's Upward Bound program and from the junior ROTC unit we have in Dayton, to inspire young people to do more and better things with the Navy and become more and more interested in it. This kind of thing we try to do to the extent possible.

Q: There's no telling how many lives that you've touched for the better as a result of your many efforts. Do you have a progress report on the Community Industry Enterprise? We talked about that a couple of years ago.

Mr. Cooper: Yes. Tomorrow morning at 8:00 o'clock, an 18-wheeler will roll up to the school and unload 80,000 spray paint cans that we're going to relabel for Borden out of Columbus. It's moving. On this job alone, we will put to work some 26 people--on a temporary basis, obviously. We can do the job in about a month. But the more of these we get in, the more we can bring the same people back. I think we're having some slight impact in terms of putting some people to work. It's moving slowly but surely.

Q: I think you started to say something that I cut off with that question.

Mr. Cooper: If I did, I've forgotten what it was.

Q: I made the point that you had undoubtedly influenced a lot of lives for the good.

Mr. Cooper: Well, I don't believe one is capable of pulling oneself up by his own bootstraps. If I've had any success in my own life, it's been because somebody helped me along the way. I therefore have a responsibility to do whatever I can to help somebody else. We can't live in this world alone.

Q: We talked earlier about religion. I think the parable of the talents applies here.

Mr. Cooper: Yes. We just can't live in this world alone. I don't know if I have that much talent. I've had an awful lot of help along the way, people who have been supportive and who have supported me, and have had a great influence in my life in terms of whatever success that I've been able to achieve. I'm eternally grateful for that, and feel that I have a responsibility to do whatever I can to pass that on to somebody else.

Q: We're right near the end of the tape. I wonder if you've got some good Dennis Nelson stories to wrap up with.

Mr. Cooper: Well, you've never lived until you've seen Dennis washing his car every day of the year, no matter whether it needed it or not, or to see Dennis decked out in one of his many uniforms, looking better than anybody you've ever seen in a naval officer's uniform. The thing I remember most about Dennis, and the thing that I'll be eternally grateful to him for is the fact that he brought us back together as a group. He was single-handedly responsible for doing that. He felt a commitment in that regard, and he worked until he accomplished it. A hell of a guy and one that you'll never forget.

Q: I wish I could have known him.

Mr. Cooper: Yes. You missed a lot by not having known Dennis.

Q: When I talked to Mrs. Nelson, she said that somebody from the Navy Archives had come out and interviewed him some years back. I have not found any trace of that. If you have any clues or hear about such a thing, I'd like to get hold of it.

Mr. Cooper: I'd be glad to contact you if I know.

Q: As before, I thank you very much. I'm a member of your fan club and grateful to you for the time that you've spent documenting this for the benefit of history.

Mr. Cooper: It's our pleasure.

Q: Thank you.

Mr. Cooper: We've enjoyed working with you and getting to know you.

Appendixes

to

Mr. George C. Cooper

Oral History

OFFICER CANDIDATE INDOCTRINATION SCHOOL
U. S. NAVAL TRAINING STATION
Great Lakes, Illinois
Camp Robert Smalls

Course Outline (1-44)

SEAMANSHIP

Instructor
Lt. (jg) F. G. Headley, USNR

Texts

Bluejackets' Manual
Modern Seamanship - Knight
Watch Officers' Guide

# OUTLINE FOR COURSE IN SEAMANSHIP
## OFFICER CANDIDATE SCHOOL
### CAMP ROBERT SMALLS

| LESSON | SUBJECT | ASSIGNMENT |
|---|---|---|
| 1 | General Characteristics of Ships | BJM - pp. 101; 175-187. |
| 2 | General Characteristics of Ships | BJM - pp. 424-427. |
| 3 | Lecture on Compartmentation Quiz | BJM - pp. 216-234. Lecture Notes and Ship Diagrams KNIGHT - pp. 28-34. |
| 4 | Boats and Boat Handling | BJM - pp. 313-315; pp. 321-338. |
| 5 | Boats and Boat Handling Quiz and Lecture | BJM - pp. 539-546; 564-578. p. 657. |
| 6 | Ship Handling | WOG - pp. 22-31. |
| 7 | Ship Handling Quiz and Lecture | WOG - pp. 39-66. |
| 8 | Ground Tackle | BJM - pp. 442-456. |
| 9 | Ground Tackle Quiz and Lecture | BJM - pp. 636-645. KNIGHT - 258-281. |
| 10 | Mooring and Ground Tackle Quiz and Lecture | BJM - pp. 432-437. KNIGHT - 298-322. |

OUTLINE FOR COURSE IN SEAMANSHIP

OFFICER CANDIDATE SCHOOL

CAMP ROBERT SMALLS

| LESSON | SUBJECT | ASSIGNMENT |
|---|---|---|
| 11 ✓ | Mooring and Ground Tackle Quiz and Lecture | KNIGHT - pp. 323-338. |
| 12 ✓ | Station Keeping and Maneuvering | KNIGHT - pp. 543-562. |
| 13 ✓ | Orders to the Wheel and Engines | KNIGHT - pp. 486-506. |
| 14 ✓ | Duties and Responsibilities of a Watch Officer Under Way Quiz and Lecture | WOG - pp. 11-21. |
| 15 | How to Abandon Ship Quiz and Lecture | Lecture Notes Only. |
| 16 | Rules of the Road | KNIGHT - pp. 339-346. WOG - pp. 31-38. |
| 17 | Rules of the Road Quiz and Lecture | BJM - pp. 579-583. KNIGHT - pp. 404-424. |
| 18 | Rules of the Road | KNIGHT - pp. 350-356. |
| 19 | Avoiding Collision Quiz and Lecture | KNIGHT - pp. 472-485. |
| 20 | Buoyage | KNIGHT - 755-757. |

OUTLINE FOR COURSE IN SEAMANSHIP

OFFICER CANDIDATE SCHOOL

CAMP ROBERT SMALLS

| LESSON | SUBJECT | ASSIGNMENT |
|---|---|---|
| 21 | Aids to Navigation<br>Quiz and Lecture | BJM - pp. 468-473;<br>pp. 584-585. |
| 22 | Flag Hoist Signaling | BJM - pp. 410-414;<br>pp. 531-535. |
| 23 | Flag Hoist Signaling<br>Quiz and Lecture | BJM - pp. 651-660.<br>WOG - 232-237. |
| 24 | Quiz | Final Quiz |

OFFICER CANDIDATE INDOCTRINATION SCHOOL
U. S. NAVAL TRAINING STATION
Great Lakes, Illinois
Camp Robert Smalls


Course Outline (1-44)


Instructor
Ensign J. W. Lowry, USNR

Texts

Navy Regulations
Naval Officers' Guide - Ageton
Watch Officers' Guide
Secnav ltr. Ser 858 13 of 27 April 1943

# OUTLINE FOR COURSE IN NAVY REGULATIONS
## OFFICER CANDIDATE SCHOOL
## CAMP ROBERT SMALLS

| LESSON | SUBJECT | ASSIGNMENT |
|---|---|---|
| 1 ✓ | Introductory; Contents of Navy Regs; Use of Index | NR - Index, Arts: $76\frac{1}{2}$ - $128\frac{1}{2}$ |
| 2 ✓ | Looking up Questions in NR | Review of Previous Assign. |
| 3 ✓ | Fitness Reports | NR - Art. 137-141<br>NOG - Ch. XIV |
| 4 ✓ | Correspondence Course | NR - Correspondence Course No. 1 |
| 5 ✓ | Quiz and Lecture | |
| 6 ✓ | Security of Information | NR - Arts. 75-, 76, 113, 114, 2003, 2039, 2040 |
| 7 ✓ | Security of Information | Same as above |
| 8 ✓ | Correspondence Course | NR - Correspondence Course No. 2 |
| 9 ✓ | Quiz and Lecture | |
| 10 ✓ | Organization and Routine of Ships and Stations | NR - Arts. 1554, 1559, Ch. 36; WOG - pp. 89-95, 125-228; NA Sec. A129-A142 B-10 |
| 11 ✓ | Organization and Routine of Ships and Stations. | |
| 12 ✓ | Correspondence Course | NR - Correspondence Course No. 3 |

# OUTLINE FOR COURSE IN NAVY REGULATIONS
## OFFICER CANDIDATE SCHOOL
### CAMP ROBERT SMALLS

| LESSON | SUBJECT | ASSIGNMENT |
|---|---|---|
| 25 | Quiz and Lecture | |
| 26 | Naval Correspondence | SECNAV ltr. Ser 85813 of April 27, 1943 |
| 27 | Naval Correspondence | Review and Exercises |
| 28 | Correspondence Course and discussion | NR - Correspondence Course No. 7 |
| 29 | Quiz and lecture | |
| 30 | Interpretation of Orders and Reporting for Duty | NR - Arts. 131-136 |
| 31 | Discussion - Interpretation of Orders and Reporting for Duty | NOG - Ch. IV |
| 32 | Correspondence Course and Discussion | NR - Correspondence Course No. 8 |
| 33 | Quiz and Lecture | |
| 34 | Movie - Reporting for Duty | |
| 35 | Responsibility for Naval Material | NR - 76, 74. |
| 36 | Correspondence Course and Discussion | NR - Correspondence Course No. 9. |

# OUTLINE FOR COURSE IN NAVY REGULATIONS
## OFFICER CANDIDATE SCHOOL
### CAMP ROBERT SMALLS

| LESSON | SUBJECT | ASSIGNMENT |
|---|---|---|
| 13 ✓ | Quiz and Lecture | |
| 14 ✓ | Watches and Watch Standing | NR - Ch. 28<br>WOG - Ch. I, II, XVIII. |
| 15 ✓ | Ship and Station Logs | Cor. Supp. to #13<br>WOG - Ch. XIX<br>NA - SECS. B-347-B-349 |
| 16 ✓ | Correspondence Course and Discussion | NR - Correspondence Course No. 4 |
| 17 ✓ | Quiz and discussion | |
| 18 ✓ | Naval Correspondence | NR - Arts. 2003, 2004, 2006, 2010, 2041, 2042. SECNAV ltr - par 1-10 |
| 19 ✓ | Naval Correspondence | NR - 2043, 699 (2,3a), 2028(2), 2031, 2021. |
| 20 | Correspondence Course and Discussion | NR - Correspondence Course No. 5 |
| 21 | Quiz and Lecture | |
| 22 | Naval Correspondence Exercises | |
| 23 | Naval Correspondence | SECNAV ltr Ser. 85813 of April 27, 1943 |
| 24 | Correspondence Course and Discussion | NR - Correspondence Course No. 6 |

OFFICER CANDIDATE INDOCTRINATION SCHOOL
U. S. NAVAL TRAINING STATION
Great Lakes, Illinois
Camp Robert Smalls

Course Outline (1-44)

GUNNERY

Instructor
Lt. W. I. Quattlebaum (Ret) USN

PROCEDURE

The course in gunnery consists of twelve (12) periods of one (1) hour over a period of twelve weeks. Since no text books are available, it is planned to devote the last fifty (50) minutes of each period to a lecture covering the subject matter listed for that period in the schedule. Lecture notes will be required and ten minute quizzes will be given at the opening of each one-hour period on the previous lecture.

Lectures will be based on "Naval Ordnance" 1939 Edition.

OUTLINE FOR COURSE IN NAVY REGULATIONS

OFFICER CANDIDATE SCHOOL

CAMP ROBERT SMALLS

| LESSON | SUBJECT | ASSIGNMENT |
|---|---|---|
| 37 | Quiz and Lecture | |
| 38 | The Bureaus | NR - Ch. 8 - 15. |
| 39 | The Bureaus | Arts. 552,- 556. |
| 40 | Correspondence Course and Discussion | NR - Correspondence Course No. 10 |
| 41 | Quiz and lecture | |
| 42 | Duties of Officers | NR - Arts. 931-951, 961, 971, 991, 998. |
| 43 | Duties of Officers | NR - Arts. 1007, 1032, 1033, 1035, 1040, 1051, 1061, 1080 |
| 44 | Correspondence Course | NR - Correspondence Courses No. 12 and 13. |
| 45 | Quiz and lecture | |
| 46 | Duties of Officers | NR - Arts. 1090, 1093, 1104, 1108, 1118, 1122, 1132, 117_, 1178, 1183, 1184, 1204. |
| 47 | Duties of Officers and Review of previous material | NR - Arts. 1208, 1234, 1244, 1245. |
| 48 | Quiz and Correspondence Course, No. 14 | NR - Correspondence Course No. 14 |

## Plan of the Week
Beginning 3/20/44 — 5 Week

### OFFICER CANDIDATE INDOCTRINATION SCHOOL
### Great Lakes Naval Training Station

| Period | Monday 20 | Tuesday 21 | Wednesday 22 | Thursday 23 | Friday 24 | Saturday 25 |
|---|---|---|---|---|---|---|
| 0600 | Reveille | | | | | |
| 0630 - 0730 | Chow | | | | | |
| 0800 | Muster by M.A.A. & Sick Call | | | | | |
| 0805 - 0910 | Drill | (Quiz) Recog. | Drill | FNS | Seamanship | Navigation |
| 0925 - 1030 | Drill | FNS | Drill | Seamanship | NR | Inspection |
| 1045 - 1150 | Drill | Navigation | Drill | Navigation | Movies | |
| 1150 - 1230 | Chow | | | | | |
| 1240 | Mast | | | | | |
| 1310 - 1415 | (Quiz) FNS | Study | (Quiz) Gunnery | Drill | Study | Gunnery |
| 1430 - 1535 | (Quiz) NR | (Quiz) Seamanship | (Quiz) Navigation | Drill | Study | Study |
| 1550 - 1655 | Exercise | Exercise | Exercise | Drill | Exercise | 1535 to 0800 Monday |
| 1700 - 1800 | Chow | | | | | |
| 1800 | Sick Call | | | | | LIBERTY |
| 1945 - 2130 | Study | Study | 1800 to 2400 | Study | Study | |
| 2230 | Taps | Taps | Liberty | Taps | Taps | |

# OUTLINE FOR COURSE IN GUNNERY
## OFFICER CANDIDATE SCHOOL
## CAMP ROBERT SMALLS

| LESSON | SUBJECT FOR DISCUSSION |
|---|---|
| 1 | Armament; armor, protective compartments. |
| 2 | Explosives; types; chemical reaction; manufacture; storage; safety precautions. |
| 3 | Ammunition; types; storage; handling; shell types; fuses |
| 4 | Major caliber guns; design; mounts; fittings; safety precautions. Turret and magazine layout, handling and loading ammunition. |
| 5 | Gunnery department organization; reports; inspections; routine tests; custody of material. |
| 6 | Fire control methods; basic fire control problem; bore sighting; fire control instruments. |
| 7 | Review of sixth week's instruction. |
| 8 | Ballistics; corrections; spotting methods; salvo pattern danger space; target designation; tactics effecting gunnery efficiency. |
| 9 | Torpedos; mines; depth charges; safety precautions; nature and cause of underwater damage. |
| 10 | Anti-air-craft fire control problems; systems of fire control; types of barrage fire; relative effectiveness. |
| 11 | Minor caliber and small arms; machine guns. |
| 12 | General review of all assignments. |

OUTLINE FOR COURSE IN NAVIGATION

OFFICER CANDIDATE SCHOOL

Camp Robert Smalls

| LESSON | SUBJECT | ASSIGNMENT |
|---|---|---|
| 1 ✓ | Introduction - Tools of the Trade. Books, Equipment, Publications, etc. | MIXTER - pp. 1 - 22 |
| 2 ✓ | Compass and Compass Errors, Types, Corrections, Problems. | MIXTER - pp. 23 - 56<br>Probs: Par. 135<br>Add. Read<br>DUTTON - pp. 35 - 77 |
| 3 ✓ | Rules of the Road<br>Radio Aids to Navigation | MIXTER - pp. 57 - 64;<br>82 - 91<br>Memorize Article 27 -<br>Rules of the Road |
| 4 ✓ | Piloting; Dead Reckoning; Mariners' Maps | MIXTER - pp. 65 - 81;<br>99 - 110<br>Additional - Read<br>DUTTON - pp. 110 - 172 |
| 5 ✓ | Review | MIXTER - pp. 111 - 114<br>and all previous readings |
| 6 ✓ | Definitions and Theory;<br>Nautical Astronomy | MIXTER - pp. 115 - 128<br>Additional - Read<br>DUTTON - pp. 173 - 197 |
| 7 ✓ | Nautical Astronomy;<br>Lines of Position from<br>Celestial Observations | MIXTER - pp. 129 - 144<br>Additional - Read<br>DUTTON - pp. 198 - 212 |
| 8 ✓ | Sextant, Altitudes and Altitude Corrections | MIXTER - pp. 146 - 162<br>Additional - Read<br>DUTTON - pp. 213 - 232 |

OFFICER CANDIDATE INDOCTRINATION SCHOOL
U. S. NAVAL TRAINING STATION
Great Lakes, Illinois
Camp Robert Smalls


Course Outline (1-44)

NAVIGATION


Instructor
Lt. Paul D. Richmond, USNR


Texts

Primer of Navigation - Mixter
Navigation and Nautical Astronomy - Dutton

OUTLINE FOR COURSE IN NAVIGATION

OFFICER CANDIDATE SCHOOL

Camp Robert Smalls

| LESSON | SUBJECT | ASSIGNMENT |
|---|---|---|
| 9 ✓ | Time, and the Chronometer | MIXTER - pp. 163 - 183<br>Additional - Read<br>DUTTON - pp. 246 - 303 |
| 10 ✓ | The Nautical Almanac and Methods of Solution of the Astronomical Triangle | MIXTER - pp. 184 - 201<br>Additional - Read<br>DUTTON - pp. 327 - 358 |
| 11 ✓ | Celestial Navigation and the Navigator's Work at Sea | MIXTER - pp. 203 - 259<br>Additional - Read<br>DUTTON - pp. 359 - 370 |
| 12 ✓ | Same as Assignment 11<br>General Review | |

*at this point we started a new course*

Index

to

Reminiscences of

Mr. George C. Cooper

Member of the Golden Thirteen

Cooper, George C.
  Boyhood in North Carolina in the 1920s and 1930s, 1-4, 74-103; parents of, 1-7, 74-82; brothers and sisters of, 1-4, 83, 87, 107-108; college education at Hampton Institute in the 1930s, 4-6, 98-99, 103-107; member of singing groups while a student at Hampton Institute, 109-111; fight with white boy in 1920s because of a racial insult, 6-7, 27; went into the sheet-metal business in North Carolina after graduation from Hampton in the late 1930s, 11-15; married Margarett Gillespie in 1939, 13; worked as a sheet-metal instructor for the National Youth Administration in Ohio in the early 1940s, 15-17; hired as civilian instructor at the naval training station, Hampton, Virginia, in 1942, 17-18, 122-124; joined the Navy as a chief petty officer in mid-1943, 19-20, 133-134; relationship with other black chief petty officers at Hampton, 129-130, 132; underwent officer training at Great Lakes, Illinois, in early 1944, 20-28, 138-173; served as personnel officer at naval training station, Hampton, Virginia, 1944-45, 28-36, 174-176; orders to the Pacific in 1945 were canceled because of a back injury incurred at Great Lakes, 35-36; Cooper was discharged from the Navy and worked at Hampton Institute as a civilian after World War II, 37, 130-131, 178; shared interests with wife Margarett, 54-56; worked in a house-cleaning business in Dayton, Ohio, in the early 1950s, 56-59; went to work as Dayton housing inspector following a case of spinal meningitis, 59-60; worked as city planner in Dayton in the 1950s, 60-61; served as director of Antioch College's international work-study program in the 1960s, 61-63; served as department director for Dayton, Ohio, city government in the 1970s and 1980s, 63; work in Dayton in the 1980s with Community Industries, Inc., to foster economic opportunities for blacks, 63-69, 188-190; Cooper's evaluation of the role of the Golden Thirteen in paving the way for later black naval officers, 69-71; enjoys jewelry-making as a hobby, 114; instances from Cooper's civilian experience in which he fostered improved racial awareness, 117-122; role with the Navy League and Navy recruiting in Dayton, Ohio, 179-180, 187-188

Cooper, Laura J.
  George Cooper's mother, a religious woman who cared about helping others, 74-76, 80-82, 86, 131; as disciplinarian in the home, 94

Cooper, Margarett Gillespie
  Married George Cooper in 1939 and went to work as school librarian in North Carolina, 13-14; shared interests with husband George, 54-56; provided support to her husband during officer training, 167

Arbor, Jesse W.
   Member of the Golden Thirteen who helped the group during the 1944 training period with aircraft identification and with his sense of humor, 38-39, 138-139, 144, 146, 158-159

Armstrong, Commander Daniel W., USNR (USNA, 1915)
   As officer in charge of Camp Robert Smalls at Great Lakes, Illinois, in early 1944, Armstrong called Cooper a troublemaker before presenting his ensign's commission, 27; had little interaction with the black officer candidates at Camp Robert Smalls, 160-162

Barnes, Phillip G.
   Member of the Golden Thirteen who was quiet, hard-working, and self-conscious while undergoing officer training in 1944, 39-40, 144

Barnes, Samuel E.
   Member of the Golden Thirteen who underwent officer training at Great Lakes in early 1944, 40-41

Baugh, Dalton L.
   Member of the Golden Thirteen who was a strong leader and took an analytical approach to problems during officer training in early 1944, 41, 144

Bethune, Mary McLeod
   Black educator who influenced Mrs. Eleanor Roosevelt during World War II concerning increased opportunities for blacks in the Navy, 10, 96

Black Naval Officers
   See Golden Thirteen; National Naval Officers Association

Camp Robert Smalls
   Site of training for the first black officer candidates at Great Lakes, Illinois, in early 1944, 20-28, 138-173

Community Industries, Inc.
   An organization developed in Dayton, Ohio, in the 1980s to foster economic opportunities for blacks, 63-69, 188-190

Cooper, Edward L.
   George Cooper's father, a North Carolina sheet-metal worker in the early years of the 20th century, inspired his children to excel, 1-7, 11-12, 80-81, 113, 115; religious interests, 74-75, 79; leadership qualities, 77-79; as disciplinarian in the home, 94; financial support for George Cooper, 111

Golden Thirteen
    Black enlisted men who were trained to be naval officers at Great Lakes, Illinois, in early 1944, 20-28, 138-173; Cooper's assessments of the individual members of the group, 38-54; role in paving the way for the many black naval officers who followed, 69-73; reunion of Golden Thirteen members on board the guided missile destroyer Kidd (DDG-993) in 1982, 71-72; role of the group in Navy recruiting in the 1980s, 72

Goodwin, Reginald E.
    Member of the Golden Thirteen who served a liaison role in early 1944 between the black officer candidates and the white leadership at Great Lakes, 42-43, 162-163

Great Lakes Naval Training Station, Great Lakes, Illinois
    See Naval Training Station, Great Lakes, Illinois

Hair, James E.
    Member of the Golden Thirteen who attended Bethune-Cookman College in the 1930s, 10; description of Hair's personality, 43-45

Hampton Institute, Hampton, Virginia
    Black college at which Cooper received education and vocational training in the 1930s, 4-6, 98-99, 103-107; had various singing groups that performed outside the school in the 1930s, 109-111; founded by Brigadier General Samuel Chapman Armstrong in 1868, 4; George Cooper and Margarett Gillespie met while students at Hampton and were married soon afterward, 55; Cooper worked on the faculty as a civilian right after World War II, 37, 130-131
    See also Naval Training Station, Hampton, Virginia

Heitger, Lieutenant Louis C., USNR
    Compassionate naval officer who served at the naval training station, Hampton, Virginia, in the mid-1940s, 149

Integration
    See Racial Integration

Kidd, USS (DDG-993)
    Guided missile destroyer that was the site of a reunion of the Golden Thirteen in 1982, 71-72

Kunde, James E.
    Dayton, Ohio, city manager who hired Cooper as a department director in the early 1970s, 63

Lear, Charles B.
    Member of the Golden Thirteen who was made a warrant boatswain in 1944 and committed suicide following World War II, 25, 169; contribution to the group during officer training, 45-46

Crawford, Cal
    Owner of a house-cleaning business in which Cooper worked in Dayton, Ohio, in the early 1950s, 56-60

Davis, Peggy Cooper
    George and Margarett Cooper's daughter, who is a professor at New York University, 132

Dille, Lieutenant John F., Jr., USNR
    White officer who provided support and inspiration to the Golden Thirteen when the group was undergoing officer training at Great Lakes, Illinois, in early 1944, 23-24, 154, 156-157; has worked in the 1980s to provide opportunities for blacks in the news media, 155

Downes, Commander Edwin H., USNR (USNA, 1920)
    As head of naval training station, Hampton, Virginia, hired Cooper as a civilian instructor in 1942, 17-18; arranged for Cooper to join the Navy as a chief petty officer in mid-1943, 19-20, 129; supportive of Cooper after a white captain expressed discomfort at meeting Cooper at Hampton after he was commissioned, 31-33, 127-128; used metal objects made in a shop at Hampton to win favors for the school when visiting Washington, D. C., 34-35; leadership qualities, 125-126, 132; notified Cooper that he was being reassigned to Great Lakes in early 1944 for what turned out to be officer training, 137-138

Education
    Cooper's father stressed to him the value of education when he was growing up in the 1920s and 1930s, 2-3, 75-76; Cooper received a mediocre education in the segregated schools in North Carolina, 3-4, 88, 92-94; Cooper's education and vocational training at Hampton Institute in the 1930s, 4-6, 98-99, 103-107; Cooper served as director of Antioch College's international work-study program in the 1960s, 61-63

FBI
    See Federal Bureau of Investigation

Federal Bureau of Investigation
    Investigation of Cooper in mid-1940s revealed neighborhood fight he had in the 1920s, 7-8, 27; Cooper resented the investigation in 1943 of black officer candidates' backgrounds, 163-166

Garvey, Marcus
    Black nationalist leader who served as a hero to black people early in the 20th century, 95

Gilliard, Joe
    Craftsman who made metal objects at the naval training station, Hampton, Virginia, in World War II, 34-35

Racial Prejudice
    Cooper fought with a white boy in Washington, North, Carolina, in the early 1920s as the result of a racial insult, 6-7, 27; a supervisor for the National Youth Administration in Ohio in the early 1940s did not believe Cooper was capable of teaching a course in sheet metal, 15-17; some instructors at the segregated officer candidate school in early 1944 took a racist attitude toward the Golden Thirteen, 22-23, 25-26, 147-148, 153-154; white sailors at naval training station, Hampton, Virginia, sometimes crossed the street in 1944-45 to avoid saluting Ensign Cooper, 29; Cooper nearly had a fight with one individual who insulted him, 30-31; a black captain who visited Hampton was quickly shipped out because of his discomfort at meeting a black officer, Cooper, 31-33, 127-128; Cooper experienced hostility from whites while working as a hotel bellhop during his high school years, 89-91; racial violence occurred in North Carolina when Cooper was growing up there, but his parents protected him from it, 101-103

Racial Segregation
    Produced mediocre education for black students in public schools in North Carolina in the 1920s and 1930s, 3-4; blacks had no choice but to accept the situation in North Carolina, 8, 99-101; in the 1930s, the Navy was an unattractive career choice for blacks before World War II because opportunities were limited, 9-10; the black officer candidates at Great Lakes, Illinois, in early 1944 were trained in segregated Camp Robert Smalls, 20-28, 138-173; even though segregation was a way of life in North Carolina in the 1920s and 1930s, Cooper's parents operated successfully in that atmosphere, 85-87; difficulties for black people travelling in the United States, 135-136

Reagan, John W.
    Member of the Golden Thirteen who brought both serenity and seriousness to the black officer training at Great Lakes in early 1944, 50-52

Religion
    Family prayer in the Cooper home in the 1920s and 1930s, 74, 85; Cooper's parents attended different churches, 75, 79, 84-85

Scotland
    The submarine tender Simon Lake (AS-33) played host to the Coopers for Black History Month while deployed to Holy Loch in February 1988, 180-187

Simon Lake, USS (AS-33)
    Submarine tender that played host to the Coopers for Black History Month while deployed to Holy Loch, Scotland, in February 1988, 180-187

Lewis, Captain Joseph D., USNR
    Navy campus liaison officer in the 1980s at Central State University, Wilberforce, Ohio, 180, 188

Martin, Graham E.
    Member of the Golden Thirteen who inspired the other black officer candidates during training at Great Lakes in early 1944, 47-48, 104

National Naval Officers Association
    An organization comprised of black naval officers who are achieving success in the Navy of the 1980s, 69

National Youth Administration
    Federal program for training young people in the early 1940s, 15-17

Naval Training Station, Great Lakes, Illinois
    Site where Cooper was appointed a chief petty officer in mid-1943, 19-20, 133-134; site of officer candidate school for the Golden Thirteen in early 1944, 20-28, 138-173

Naval Training Station, Hampton, Virginia
    Site of training for black enlisted men in World War II, 17-20, 122-124; Cooper's relationships with fellow black chief petty officers, 129-130; Cooper served as personnel officer in 1944-45, 28-36, 174-176; white naval officers were sent to the naval training station at Hampton in World War II to learn about dealing with black personnel, 31-33, 127-128
    See also Hampton Institute

Navy League
    Cooper's work with the organization in Dayton, Ohio, in the 1970s and 1980s, 179-180, 187-188

Nelson, Dennis D. II
    Member of the Golden Thirteen who was bright, brash, and flamboyant during the officer training at Great Lakes in early 1944, 48-50, 158, 190-191

Officer Candidate School
    Members of the Golden Thirteen received officer training in segregated Camp Robert Smalls at Great Lakes, Illinois, in early 1944, 20-28, 138-173

Racial Integration
    While at the naval training station, Hampton, Virginia, in 1944-45, Ensign Cooper fostered situations for enlightening white sailors in the ship's company, 29-30; the role of the Golden Thirteen in fostering opportunities for future black naval officers, 69-73; instances from Cooper's civilian experience in which he fostered improved racial awareness, 117-122

Smalls, Robert
    Escaped slave for whom the training camp for black personnel was named at Great Lakes, Illinois, in World War II, 21
    See also Camp Robert Smalls

Segregation
    See Racial Segregation

Sublett, Frank E., Jr.
    Member of the Golden Thirteen who was friendly and helpful to his fellow officer candidates during training at Great Lakes in early 1944, 52-53

Training
    Sheet-metal course conducted by the National Youth Administration in Ohio in the early 1940s, 15-17; naval training station, Hampton, Virginia, provided practical training for black enlisted men during World War II, 17-20, 122-124; the Golden Thirteen received officer training at segregated Camp Robert Smalls at Great Lakes, Illinois, in early 1944, 20-28, 138-173; Community Industries, Inc., of Dayton, Ohio, provides training to blacks in the 1980s to enhance their economic opportunities, 63-69

Washington, Booker T.
    Black educator at Tuskegee Institute early in the 20th century, 96

White, William Sylvester
    Member of the Golden Thirteen who had a profound, serious approach to matters during black officer training at Great Lakes in early 1944, 53-54

Witt, FTBC (SS) Glen, USN
    Recruiter who worked with Cooper in the 1980s on programs in Dayton, Ohio, and helped set up a trip to Scotland for black history month in 1988, 180-182, 184-185

www.ingramcontent.com/pod-product-compliance
Lightning Source LLC
Chambersburg PA
CBHW080614170426
43209CB00007B/1424